Graphic Design for Electronic Documents and User Interfaces

ACM Press

Editor-in-Chief:

Peter Wegner, *Brown University*

ACM Press books represent a collaboration between the Association for Computing Machinery (ACM) and Addison-Wesley Publishing Company to develop and publish a broad range of new works. These works generally fall into one of four series.

Frontier Series. Books focused on novel and exploratory material at the leading edge of computer science and practice.

Anthology Series. Collected works of general interest to computer professionals and/or society at large.

Tutorial Series. Introductory books to help nonspecialists quickly grasp either the general concepts or the needed details of some specific topic.

History Series. Books documenting past developments in the field and linking them to the present.

In addition, ACM Press books include selected conference and workshop proceedings.

Graphic Design for Electronic Documents and User Interfaces

Aaron Marcus
Aaron Marcus and Associates

ACM Press
New York, New York

Addison-Wesley Publishing Company
Reading, Massachusetts • Menlo Park, California
New York • Don Mills, Ontario • Wokingham, England
Amsterdam • Bonn • Sydney • Singapore • Tokyo
Madrid • San Juan • Milan • Paris

ACM Press Tutorial Series.

Many of the designations used by manufacturers and sellers to distinguish their products are claimed as trademarks. Where those designations appear in this book, and Addison-Wesley was aware of a trademark claim, the designations have been printed in initial caps or all caps.

The programs, applications, and recommendations presented in this book have been included for their instructional value. They have been tested with care, but are not guaranteed for any particular purpose. Neither the author nor the publisher offer any warranties or representations, nor do they accept any liabilities with respect to the programs, applications, or recommendations.

With regard to the information and advice provided in this book, the author shall not be liable for any acts or omissions except when such acts or omissions are due to their willful misconduct or culpable negligence. The reader agrees to hold the author and his firm Aaron Marcus and Associates free and harmless from any obligation, costs, claims, judgments, attorneys' fees, and attachments arising from the advice rendered except due to the willful misconduct or culpable negligence of the author as determined in court.

ISBN 0–201–54364–8
1 2 3 4 5 6 7 8 9 10-MA-9594939291

Dedication

To my parents, Nathan Marcus and Libbie Burstein Marcus, of Omaha, Nebraska, who encouraged my interest in science and visual communications.

Preface

Computers enable everyone to layout, edit, display, and publish not only type, but graphics of all kinds: charts, maps, diagrams, photos, and illustrations. Computer graphics uses more graphic symbolism and color than ever before and even includes animation in screen display. To produce these computer graphics is one achievement; to communicate the facts, concepts, and emotional values is another. To be successful, computer graphics must communicate visually in an effective manner.

This book will advise developers and users of computer graphics-based electronic documents and interfaces, of publications, presentations, and displays, professionals, students, and general readers will learn how to communicate more effectively, whether the medium is paper, film, or glass. Based on twenty-plus years of the author's experience, the book's content provides useful guidance for every kind of hardware, software, application, and user/viewer.

Graphic Design for Electronic Documents and User Interfaces is written for people who need information now:

- Computer programmers and others who design computer-generated displays.

- Graphic designers and others responsible for the display of graphics and texts on the page.

- Executives, managers, and clerical staff who use typographic and graphics communications in their work with computers.

- Technical writers, trainers, and academics who must communicate complex information to both professional and general readers.

- Scientists, engineers, attorneys, and medical professionals who must communicate large amounts of complex data to their peers or to general audiences.

Among application areas that can benefit from this information are the following:

Artificial intelligence
CAD/CAM/CAE
Computer-based instruction
Database retrieval systems
Graphic arts and design
Executive information systems
Financial systems
Geographic information systems
Medical systems
Printing and publishing
Process control
Scientific visualization
Software engineering
Technical documentation

This book will introduce terminology, principles, guide-lines, and case studies for using information-oriented, systematic graphic design in electronic documents and user interfaces. Electronic publishing designers who are responsible for the design of printed reports and newsletters, slides, overheads, and interactive presentations will find advice on layout, text presentation, and the design of charts and diagrams. Designers of user interfaces who are responsible for the design of graphical user interface components and application data display will find useful information for the design of icons, color sets, control panels and dialogue boxes, and navigational devices that are not sufficiently prescribed by window-management or dialogue-management systems.

Readers will discover resources for existing knowledge, immediately useful advice, and potential research topics. They will learn techniques for making displays more intelligible, functional, aesthetic, and marketable.

This book covers perceptual, conceptual, and communication issues in typography, symbol systems, color, spatial composition, animation, and sequencing. This practical tutorial in graphic design will enable readers to understand what challenges lay ahead in displaying computer graphics effectively and how to achieve successful results when developing products and services.

Aaron Marcus
Emeryville, California

Contents

Graphic Design for Electronic Documents and User Interfaces

Introduction

Computer-based systems facilitate the creation and distribution of electronically published documents such as the following:

Books
Reports
Newsletters
Brochures
Posters and announcements
Slide and overhead presentations
CRT or video presentations

The applications, or software, that enables the editing and management of these documents relies on a user interface to facilitate command-control and documentation of the applications' as these functions affect data and displays.

Information-oriented, systematic graphic design can assist developers and users who are engaged in electronic publishing and user-interface design by improving visual communication. In addition to making design and production more efficient, well designed text and graphics can help products and services reach the proper audience to give readers or viewers information, to provide aesthetic pleasure, and, where appropriate, to persuade the reader or viewer. Designing successful publications and user interfaces requires that designers consider three issues: development, usability, and acceptance.

Development includes the following considerations. In each one of these areas, graphic design can help achieve successful communication objectives:

Constraints for appearance on paper, film, glass
Design and production tools
Available libraries of templates and clip art
Support for rapid prototyping
Customizability

Usability typically includes the following considerations. Again, graphic design can assist:

Legibility
Product identity
Clear conceptual model
Multiple formats

Acceptance factors includes the following considerations. Once again, improved visual communication can have a positive impact:

Installed base
Corporate identity
International markets
Documentation and training
Readability

A primary technique to achieve improved visual communication is to use clear, distinct, consistent visible language. Visible language refers to all the verbal and visual signs that convey meaning to a viewer. A fundamental concept is that it is possible to set up explicit rules, specifications, and guidelines for visible language that affect electronic publications or user interfaces. The chapters of this book are organized into categories of visible language.

Layout refers to formats, proportions and grids, and to two- and three-dimensional composition.

Typography refers to selection of typefaces and typesetting. Typical typeface examples include variable-width sans serif and serif fonts as well as fixed-width fonts of the kind found on simple printers and screen displays. Typical typesetting arrangements include texts, tables and lists, and forms.

Color, texture, and light play an increasingly important role in conveying complex information and portraying a three-dimensional reality.

Symbolism includes all kinds of signs, icons, and symbols, from the photographically real to the abstract. Because advanced electronic publications have increasing display capability, every aspect of imagery must be well designed.

Charts, diagrams, and maps include the specialized constructions of text and graphics to convey complex structures and processes.

Screen design includes all of the appearance characteristics of windows, menus, icons, cursors, control panels, and dialogue boxes for interactive systems.

For each section of this book, the reprinted articles provide an explanation of terms, basic design principles, specific recommendations, case studies, and references to other resource material. The material presented here can be a useful guide to professional practice as well as to research and development activities.

As more computer graphics systems move toward color display, the industry will gradually produce more high-quality, appropriate literature for developers and users. In the last few years a number of new publications have appeared that provide practical advice. This trend can be expected to continue.

Chapter 1   **Layout**

One of the fundamental challenges to designers of effective visual communication is how to lay elements out in space, especially two-dimensional space. In some cases, designers must plan layouts for three-dimensional space as well.

One example of three-dimensional layout is the "realistic" shadows, highlights, and textured surfaces of graphical user interfaces with layered windows, control panels, and dialogue boxes. A more compelling situation is the wrap-around three-dimensional space of artificial, or virtual, realities provided by the computer graphic display environments manufactured by such firms as VPL Research of Redwood City, California, and AutoDesk of Sausalito, California.

1.1 Proportion and Grids: Invisible Keys to Successful Layout

Introduction

When it comes to the complex information displayed on computer screens, and traditionally and electronically published documents, behind every good layout stands a grid: quiet but forceful. A layout grid is a set of horizontal and vertical lines that divide the visual field into units that have visual and conceptual integrity. For example, the pages of this book are broken up into columns of text and illustrations with an area at the top, called the header, containing the name of the publication and the page number.

The grid is an aid to the visible language programmer or graphic designer when determining page or screen composition. The reader or viewer is usually unaware of its presence, but the grid contributes to the legibility and readability of all visual presentations. In this chapter, some of the principles that determine layout grids, such as proportion, format, text type, and illustration, are discussed.

Proportion

Every age and every culture has had its favorite proportional relationships. The relationship of the length to the width of the Greek Parthenon on the Acropolis expressed an ideal of beauty in classical Greek architecture. What constitutes beauty in European, Japanese, or Hindu classical architecture may vary, and the aesthetic of an age may transform itself, as we witness in the legacy of architectural styles in Europe. However, a certain set of relationships has found continuing expression in the designed environment of many cultures and across a variety of visual forms, from architecture and painting to typeface design and page layout. It is appropriate to review some of the basic proportions as shown in Fig.1.1.

In the first row of this figure, the rectangles depict typical classical proportions used in graphic design, industrial design, and architectural design across many cultures and over many centuries. The second row shows modern proportions used in industrial practice.

The square is the simplest proportion. The square established within any visual field is an attention-getting shape and suggests stability and permanence. When rotated on its diagonal, it becomes very dynamic, suggesting movement and tension. The shape even acquires a different name: the diamond. Although square screens are not produced, a square format for layout of all contents can be established. Square-cut pages are not usually economical for books, but are occasionally used. The square format for the total visual field achieves a commanding presence.

Visually, the square-root of two proportion has within it an inscribed square that may be used as a natural division

Figure 1.1 Classical and
Modern Proportions

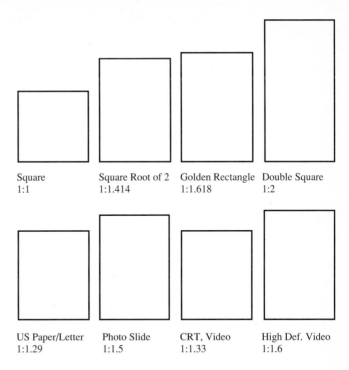

Square   Square Root of 2   Golden Rectangle Double Square
1:1   1:1.414   1:1.618   1:2

US Paper/Letter   Photo Slide   CRT, Video   High Def. Video
1:1.29   1:1.5   1:1.33   1:1.6

of the rectangle. If the rectangle is divided equally in two along its length, it forms two smaller rectangles, each of which is a square-root of two rectangle. This property occurs only with this rectangular proportion and makes this shape an ideal format for book pages. When the book is opened to a two-page spread, the entire layout has the same outside proportion as the individual page. This technique has been utilized in traditional European and Japanese book design. In fact, the square-root of two has been adopted as the basis for European paper size standards. This means that typical booklet, magazine, letterhead, and poster formats appear in this proportion.

The rectangle whose sides have a proportion of 1:1.618, known as the golden proportion, has intrigued artists, designers, and philosophers since antiquity. A mathematical relationship exists between this proportion and growth patterns in plant and animal life. Greek architecture utilized this proportion, and the early twentieth century French architect LeCorbusier made the proportion the basis for his modular system of architectural elements. The golden rectangle has the unique property that an inscribed square, which may be used to divide the rectangle naturally, leaves a remaining area whose sides are also of the golden rectangle proportion. This process of subdivision can be continued indefinitely.

Although not well known to Westerners, the double square is a familiar proportion in Japan. For example, the Japanese tatami mat used for traditional floor covering is manufactured with this proportion. For rectangles more elongated than the double square, it becomes increasingly difficult to sense the distinctiveness of the shape established by the proportion.

These basic rectangular proportions can be used to establish the outer boundary of a visual field, a major component of the visual field, or smaller areas used for illustrations or text blocks. Examples of typical visual compositions include a chart, a form, or a text and illustration grouping as it is established on a page layout, within a presentation slide, or for the user interface of a screen display.

Formats

In using these visually strong proportions, one must be aware that many of the typical rectangles encountered in business and information displays do not appear in the above recommended proportions. Figure 1.1 also provides formats or outer boundaries of visual fields in common commercial or industrial products.

Note that only the newly proposed wide-screen high-definition television format is close to the traditional proportions. In accommodating these nontraditional proportions, a designer typically establishes a major subdivision of the format that uses one of the classical stronger proportions. For example, a horizontal slide chart may appear divided unequally with a square area on the right for the main title and data display and the remaining area at the left for legend and charting units.

The lack of correspondence among these modern display proportions implies, at the very least, that visual compositions must have sufficient margins around the four edg-

Figure 1.2
Page Layout Grid

The grid lines indicate locations and/or maximum ex-
tents of columns of text,
titling, and illustrations.

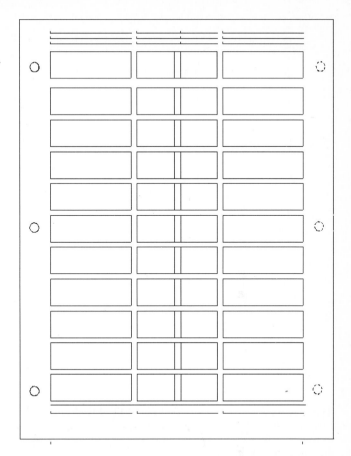

es so that the composition can be easily used in several
media. In fact, the four outer margin indicators form an
initial set of lines for almost any spatial layout grid.
This does not mean that color areas or portions of symbolism never appear in the margins; however, it does
imply that these elements may be trimmed off if the
composition must be used in a medium other than its
original creation.

Bindings of books, magazines, notebooks, etc., provide
an additional consideration (see Fig. 1.2) when determining the margin at the binding edge. Some documentation
pages, for example, allow for the possibility of
three-hole punching for inclusion in notebooks (with a
margin of no less than 5/8 inch).

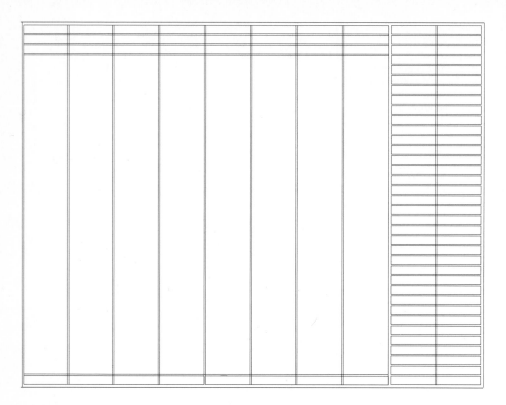

Figure 1.3
Screen Layout Grid

The grid lines indicate locations and/or maximum extents of windows, status bars, titles, scroll bars, pop-up dialog boxes or control panels, etc.

One screen layout consideration (see Fig. 1.3) that many office automation and electronic publishing workstations employ in partitioning the high-resolution display (60 to 150 pixels per inch, or ppi) is the need to display a standard letterhead sheet. In many cases, the width of a vertical page is maintained at actual size, while a small portion of the depth of the page is hidden because of the limits of resolution (1024 pixels of depth means 10.24 inches can be shown, not 11 inches for 100 ppi displays). Typically, the remaining area of the display at the right of a horizontal screen is used for the command and control menus, status displays, etc.

Text Type

Most screen and page layout grids have multiple columns. How are the column widths determined? The first considerations are what size text type will be used and what constitutes a reasonable length of characters in a line. Typically, 40 to 60 characters maximum deter-mine primary column widths, whether or not the lines are set unjustified (ragged right). The columns are separated by spaces, called gutters, that are at least two characters wide (and in printed matter 1 to 2 picas wide, where a pica is approximately 1/6 inch). Typically, two to five columns can be accommodated in a vertical or horizontal page or screen width. Sometimes, one major text column dominates the right side of the format, while a narrower column at the left is used for comments, subtitles, or margin notes.

Horizontal grid lines break up the columns into zones for running heads, primary titling, main text, and footnotes. There are several methods of determining where to place text with respect to these horizontal lines. One of the most consistent approaches is to assume that the horizontal lines indicate positions on which lines of type would sit. A typical approach to spacing is to skip one line of type whenever spatial emphasis is required, for example, before a subhead. This approach provides consistent alignment of most text type across the page or screen and from page to page or screen to screen.

Text areas need "breathing space" around them. One of the typical oversights of screen layout, especially in multiwindow display, is that text areas within windows often have no empty outer margins. Text from one window will run directly into the dividing line between windows and the text of another window. This approach to layout makes the screen look unnecessarily cramped and cluttered. A simple solution, even with displays using typographic characters with fixed widths, is to keep the contents of the window one character space from the window border. Unlike page layout, screens usually appear less complicated when a single thin line separates windows from each other rather than two lines separated by space. This effect occurs because it is not easy to display a very thin line on the screen.

Illustrations

Considerations of typical illustrations, whether the figures are photographic, diagrammatic, or textual, may help to determine column widths and the placement of horizontal and vertical lines used to define the typical areas of illustrations. The horizontal lines are usually separated by one skipped text line. In fact, one of the most useful aspects of the layout grid is its ability to provide both variation and consistency to the size, proportion, and location of illustrations.

By using a limited number of small rectangular areas determined by vertical column lines and the horizontal lines (see Fig. 1.3), it is possible to set up a pleasing visual rhythm that accounts for the practical requirements of space for each illustration. The figures themselves may be outlined with thin rectangles that represent part of the grid, or they may be displayed with a light gray background to indicate the portion of the page or screen.

Conclusion

Proportion, format, text type, and illustration are not individually responsible for the visual relationships established in the layout grid of pages, slides, screens, or even for icons or symbols (see Fig. 1.4). Usually, the visible language programmer or graphic designer must balance a number of these factors to resolve the different needs of text, figures, and format. Yet, each of these considerations can contribute to a rational solution that allows room for personal preferences and, at the same time, enhance the display of information. A more detailed discussion of proportion, grids, and layout can be found in Mueller-Brockman's book *Grid Systems in Graphic Design* and in other references cited in the Bibliography, Section 1.1.

1.2 Graphic Design of Spatial Metaphors, Displays, and Tools

Introduction

From the very beginning of computer technology, electronic publications and user interfaces have appear-ed as spatial images, although their spatial features were not necessarily complex or explicitly recognized by users. All text and nonverbal signs appearing in a virtual space were understood as a single flat plane of symbols.

Current technology of high-performance workstations permits any element of the display to appear as dynamic, polychrome, three-dimensional signs in a three-dimensional space. A NASA conference on spatial

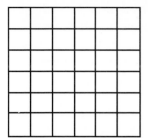

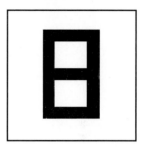

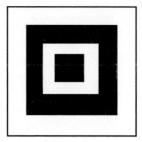

Figure 1.4 Grid-Based
Symbol Design

The grid indicates lines
for alignment, maximum
extent, and orientation of
parts of the symbol.

displays and spatial instruments pointed out the rich set
of disciplines that can contribute to issues of spatial
presentations (see Section 1.3). The complexity of appearance and the user's interaction with the display
provide significant challenges to the graphic designer
of current and future user interfaces and information
graphics. In particular, spatial depiction provides many
opportunities for effective communication of objects,
structures, processes, navigation, selection, and manipulation. The following discussion presents issues that
are relevant to optimizing spatial attributes for effective
visual communication.

**Current Spatial
Approaches**

Influenced by the introduction of the Xerox Star and
Apple Macintosh computers in the early 1980s,
computer graphics programmers have emphasized the
multiwindowed desktop spatial metaphor as a basis for
appearance and interaction. The viewer is looking at a
flat background, with one or more rectangular windows
in front of the background plane. The windows may tile
the foreground or may overlap in various ways. Icons, or
other small signs, standing for objects, processes, structures, or data, can appear on the background plane or in
the window planes. In addition to windows, which may
show deep spatial scenes, various menus and dialogue

boxes can appear within windows or in front of all the windows. In front of all these elements, cursors may float across the visual field. Any of the windows or any part of the background may contain graphics images that depict a deep three-dimensional space.

The space is designed as a shallow layering of foreground, middle ground, and background, reminiscent of traditionally shallow spatial compositions in modern painting. This multiple-layered composition is also reminiscent of layered cartoon animation cells, a kind of 2 1/2-dimensional space as it is sometimes called. Certain visual enhancements to the depiction of objects in this space are used typically to help the viewer understand the spatial composition. These enhancements include the following techniques:

Drop shadows
Beveled edges
Highlighting and lowlighting
Shrinking and growing

Drop shadows, for example, typically directed to the lower-right corner of the display, help to convey the layering of windows, pull down or pop-up (more accurately pop-in-front-of) menus, or dialogue boxes. In some user interfaces, icons, buttons, switches, menu elements, or entire rectangles of menus, dialogue boxes, or windows may be given beveled sides so that they appear to protrude toward the viewer. Sometimes their sides are colored with varying levels of gray value to strengthen the illusion of three-dimensional form and a light source, often implied to be located at the upper-left corner of the display. In addition, entire windows or other areas of the screen may be highlighted to stand out to the viewer, while other windows may be lowlighted to suggest that they are further back in space. Elements sometimes change their size and appearance; for example, an icon may be enlarged to become a window. This change is often shown as a spatial growth in two dimensions, which contributes to the illusion of overlapping elements.

These techniques are similar to those employed by
designers to enhance information-oriented graphics,
such as the design of charts, maps, and diagrams.
These spatial qualities have distinct communication
value from a graphic design point of view and accomplish the following:

• Distinguish various elements on the screen

• Help the viewer to recognize particular classes
  of objects

• Add charm or appeal to the design style of the
  user interface

• Convey corporate or product design conventions

Besides the traditional desktop, the image of the control
panel is also used in some user interfaces, in which the
entire screen may convey one or more flat panels with
switches, knobs, and other control devices. A variant on
the desktop is the giant desktop in which the viewer
sees one part of the background through a viewport and
must use scrolling devices to examine other areas of the
background. Another variant of the desktop might be
called the multiple desktop in which the viewer may
move from desktop to desktop by zooming, sudden cuts
or pops, or other visual techniques. A memorable approach using sound cues to aid spatial cues was presented by the MIT Architecture Machine Group's spatial
database-management system in the 1970s in which the
background plane zoomed toward the viewer with an
audible "whoosh" and "pop" as the viewer suddenly
dropped onto a layer below with an audible popping
sound. More recently, hypertext products generally use
the notion of the screen as one or more planes or cards
that can be scrolled or panned.

**Other Spatial
Metaphors**

Programmers have experimented with other spatial
metaphors to facilitate human-computer communication. One alternative is the metaphor of architecture.
The Learning Company, for example, began offering in

the early 1980s a children's game called Rocky's Boots that provides the viewer with the metaphor of a set of rooms, each with entrances and exits. The screen display communicates a set of spaces linked by the topology of familiar architectural experiences.

Other approaches are possible as workstations provide ever greater capabilities to manipulate three-dimensional reality. With the advent of displays supporting complex imagery based on Adobe's Display PostScript picture-definition language, as in products from Sun and NeXT, it is possible to display screen metaphors that are more sophisticated visually, metaphors that use the building or even the urban environment as a basis for spatial communication of the user interface. All that is required is a set of familiar symbols, a familiar spatial arrangement, and a familiar ritual for interacting with the symbols. For years, video-games have employed a variety of spatial idioms, including rooms, buildings, and landscapes to convey the field of action.

Future Directions

Within the entertainment field and within current user-interface design, future directions of spatial representation are already emerging. Two areas of emphasis are depictions of deep space and depictions of three-dimensional objects.

In commercial cable and broadcast television and within the film industry, there has been a continuous fascination with depictions of deep space. The title sequence of the movie *Star Wars* inherits a tradition from older films. Today, it is routine for evening news programs, weather reports, movie introductions, and station-identification breaks to feature photographic images, typography, and other elements swirling about within deep spatial representations. For several years, NASA experimented with a head-mounted display in which a complete three-dimensional environment was continuously depicted to the viewer. Recent commercial products offer their versions of virtual three-dimensional experiences.

Currently, the depictions of dynamic objects and of surfaces with projected light and cast shadows are very expensive to produce, requiring significant budgets, time, personnel, and equipment. The creators of sophisticated animation software, however, like Wavefront of Santa Barbara, California, are broadening the base of hardware and user groups, so that the computer graphics industry will be nurtured with more powerful spatial-display and image-rendering capabilities. Eventually these capabilities will be routinely available for widespread use in the depiction of user-interface components. Even without expensive workstations, it is possible to display three-dimensional objects as components of the user interface. A music-editing software package produced in the late 1980s for the Commodore Amiga, for example, showed solid pillars framing the sides of and a proscenium arch over the score of a musical composition.

Spatial Depth Cues

In all user interfaces and information graphics, there is a need to present data objects, processes, their status, and structures of various kinds. In addition, the designer must determine means for enabling the user to navigate, select, and manipulate these objects in various ways. Designers may find it useful to review Gibson's list of visual cues that establish the perception of space. These perspective experiences are taken from Edward Hall's *The Hidden Dimension* (see Section 1.3).

Position

Texture: gradual increase in density of texture of a receding surface

Size: gradual decrease in size of distant objects

Linear perspective: parallel lines receding to vanishing points

Parallax

Binocular perspective: an image with shifted object locations for each eye

Motion perspective: objects moving at uniform speeds appear slower if distant

Cues independent of the position and motion of the viewer

Aerial perspective: increased haziness and bluish color with distance

Blur: objects nearer or more distant than the focal plane appear fuzzy

Vertical location: lower part appears nearer, the upper part farther away

Shift of texture or linear spacing: abrupt changes appear as depth shifts

Shift in double imagery: in distant views, nearer objects have doubling gradient

Shift in rate of motion: close objects move much more than distant objects

Completeness or continuity of outline: nearer objects overlap others

Shift of light and dark: abrupt changes appear as edges, gradual changes as roundness

Some, but not all, of these cues are currently employed within user interfaces and information graphics to create convincing spatial images. As user interfaces and dynamic information graphics become more complex visually, designers will utilize more of these depth cues and consequently will need to determine the listed spatial depiction attributes in a systematic manner.

Relation to Product or Industrial Design

In addition to more complex spatial metaphors that unite objects in a unified space, increased sophistication of spatial imagery also means that the individual components of the user interface can take on elaborate internal spatial composition. For example, all of the typical user interface components, such as windows, menus, dialogue boxes, icons, and cursors, can acquire significant three-dimensional qualities. Consider the following possible examples.

• Windows with solid-shaped extrusions for title bars and scroll bars.

• Scroll bars appearing as translucent round columns with the visible portion of the screen as a solid tube within.

• Windows as the front surface of rectangular parallelepipeds, with regular semantics conventions assigned to the other faces of the solid window.

• Icons as three-dimensional blocks with internal moving parts, whose surface characteristics (metallic, rough, warm, etc.) or interlocking features might contribute to its denotation.

• Cursors as large, three-dimensional portraits whose pointing fingertips focus the user's attention on a particular screen component while their facial expression conveys important connotative content.

At this point, user-interface designers would benefit by examining the history and current practice of professionals in graphic design, architecture, industrial design, and product design. In contemporary industrial design, for example, one finds a dialectic taking place between minimalist approaches in which all objects have a closely synchronized, limited selection of attributes, and the more exuberant approaches in which eclectic, exotic, wildly different attributes appear. Design at this point leaves the engineering domain and enters the world of aesthetic styling, which contributes significantly to the marketing of products worldwide. It is also in this realm of user interfaces and information graphics as plastic, shaped artifacts that corporate design or product design standards influence the three-dimensional design task (see Fig. 1.5).

As user interfaces and information graphics take on more spatial attributes, for example, in virtual or artificial realities, the collection of symbols in space take on cultural characteristics far more complicated than the straightforward issues of ergonomics. It would seem reasonable for user interface and informational graphic designers to consider the discipline of proxemics, the science of interpersonal space (pioneered by Edward Hall), for guidance in user-computer spaces.

Conclusion

Aided by advancing technology and spurred both by the need for depicting increasing amounts of data and functions and by market interest, user interfaces and information graphics are taking on more spatial characteristics. To achieve communication effectiveness, user-interface and information-graphics designers will need to coordinate, unify, and optimize a very broad, deep hierarchy of spatial attributes for every component of image. Lessons can be learned by examining the challenges and achievements of professionals in other disciplines working with complex spatial structures, both as matters of geometry and as cultural artifacts. The scope and rate of change within user-interface and information-graphics design promises to offer an exciting opportunity and test of skill for the human mind in shaping three-dimensional communicative forms.

1.3 An Annotated Bibliography for Graphic Design of Spatial Displays

Introduction

Much of the recent technological development in computer graphics has emphasized the display of sophisticated three-dimensional imagery on personal computers as well as high-end specialized workstations. Spatial images increasingly find their way into buttons and switches of user interfaces and into computer-aided design/manufacturing/electronics engineering (CAD/CAM/CAE) depictions of objects of all kinds. The conference "Spatial Displays and Spatial Instruments" sponsored by NASA Ames Research Center in California and the University of California at Berkeley testifies to the interest in this subject by many disciplines, from psychology to engi-

Figure 1.5 Sketch for a Three-Dimensional User Interface

The screen shows non-horizontal menus, graphics editing tools placed in a three-dimensional background, three-dimensional control panels, curvilinear status messages, triangular "system busy" pattern, and news-wire running titlebar component.

neering (see reference to Ellis below). The increased use of spatial displays and spatial objects in computer graphics sys-tems creates a need for effective visual display among the community of professionals who are graphically editing or viewing the contents of these spatial images.

Developers and users will need to make sophisticated decisions about the use of typography, symbols and pictograms, color, layout, illustration, animation effects, and sequencing of information to produce optimum spatial effects.

Traditionally, professional animators and graphic designers have made these decisions about the visible language of spatial images. The responsibility now falls upon the developer or user of computer graphics systems. As in other areas of computer-assisted graphic display, the software often cannot automatically select the correct orientation or colors or then apply them properly.

In a few cases, libraries of shapes, organizing structures, or color templates for a limited variety of applications may exist, but in most cases the quality of the final design will depend upon the experience, imagination, and skill of the developer or user. There are a number of references that provide excellent advice on issues, principles, recommendations, and examples of fine spatial design to guide the neophyte. These references are not usually located in one part of a library or in one kind of bookstore. It may take some effort to locate them. In our firm, we have built up a library of some of the better spatial-design publications written over the past 20 years. Some of these publications are now quite old, but they are still relevant to the needs of people who are trying to get the highest visual-communication quality out of computer graphics systems. Major reference books and journals on architecture, industrial design, psychology of vision, geometry, and topology are not included, because these resources are readily available in libraries and bookstores.

I strongly suggest that you secure some of these publications for your own reference library, or at least examine them in art and design libraries. I also recommend examining some of the other works listed in this book because spatial image design includes complex decisions about typography, color, and symbolism as well. This list includes not only books on the subject but also certain articles, pamphlets, booklets, and magazines. Many of the art and design publications may be ordered from specialized book sellers, particularly Wittenborn Books, 1018 Madison Avenue, New York, NY 10021, or from ordering services such as Print Books, 6400 Goldsboro Road, Bethesda, MD 20817-9969.

Recommended Publications

Berkman, Aaron, *Art and Space*, Social Sciences Publishers, New York, 1949, 175 pp. A review of spatial organization in Western painting, with 32 plates and 38 figures.

Bertin, Jacques, *Semiology of Graphics*, trans. W.J. Berg, The University of Wisconsin Press, Madison,

1983, ISBN 0-299-09060-4, 415 pp. Bertin's classic analysis of graphic sign systems presents useful information on visual coding techniques with many spatial diagram examples.

Bolt, Richard A., *The Human Interface: Where People and Computers Meet*, Lifetime Learning Publications, Wadsworth International, Belmont, CA, 1989, ISBN 0-534-03380-6, 113 pp. The text reviews the spatial database management system and other projects of the MIT Architecture Machine Group.

Critchlow, Keith, *Order in Space*: *A Design Source Book*, Studio Book, Viking Press, New York, 1970, ISBN 670-52830-7, 120 pp. The author reviews space-filling polygonal patterns and discusses their polyhedral correlates. Clearly drawn figures show construction details for all examples. This kind of book is a basic reference for two- and three-dimensional design courses.

Ellis, Stephen R., ed., *Proceedings,* Spatial Displays and Spatial Instruments Conference, NASA Conference Publication, 1989. At this conference sponsored by NASA Ames Research Center and the University of California at Berkeley, 31 August 1987, in Asilomar, CA, professionals from many disciplines discussed issues of portraying and understanding spatial images. Copies are available through Stephen R. Ellis, Mail Stop 239-3, NASA Ames Research Center, Moffett Field, CA 94035.

Ghyka, Matila, *The Geometry of Art and Life*, Sheed and Ward, New York, 1946, 174 pp. The author presents detailed mathematical, historical, and cultural information about proportion, planar geometry, and geometrical shapes in space.

Gould, Laura, and William Finzer, *Programming by Rehearsal*, Tech. report SCL-84-1, Xerox Palo Alto Research Center, May 1984, 133 pp. A shorter version appears in *Byte* 9, no. 6, June 1984. The authors present a proposal for user-interface spatial metaphor using the image of the theater proscenium.

Gregory, Richard L., *The Intelligent Eye*, McGraw-Hill, New York, 1970, LC-72-97117, 191 pp. A noted expert reviews perceptual and cognitive aspects of vision, with references to spatial vision and examples of anaglyphs.

——, *Eye and Brain: The Psychology of Seeing*, World University Library, McGraw-Hill, New York, 1968, LC 64-66178, 251 pp. A noted expert reviews perceptual and cognitive spects of vision.

Hall, Edward T., *The Hidden Dimension*, Anchor Books, New York, 1982, ISBN 0-385-08476-5, 217 pp. An anthropologist examines the human use of public and private spaces. This introduction to proxemics, the science of spatial meaning, contains many fascinating references and concludes with a summary of Gibson's 13 principles of spatial depth cueing.

——, *The Silent Language*, Fawcett World Library, New York, 1963, 192 pp. The author introduces the concept of the vocabulary of culture, with a special chapter on space.

Hambidge, Jay, *The Elements of Dynamic Symmetry,* Dover Publications, New York, 1967, LC 66-30210, 113 pp. The author presents a theory of aesthetic design based on proportion and finds its application in classic Greek design.

Herdeg, Walter, ed., *Graphis Diagrams*, Graphis Press, Zurich, 1981, ISBN 3-85709-410-9, 205 pp. The author presents many well-designed spatial charts, maps, and diagrams. A second, revised edition of this publication has also appeared.

Ivins, William M., Jr., *Art and Geometry: A Study in Space Intuitions*, Dover Publications, New York, 1946, LC 64-156511, 113 pp. The author explains the differences in space intuitions between classical Greek and Renaissance painters and sculptors.

Jencks, Charles, and William Chaitkin, *Architecture Today*, Harry N. Abrams, New York, 1982, ISBN 0-8109-0669-04, 359 pp. The authors' well-illustrated text reviews current stylistic trends in contemporary architecture.

Lakoff, George, and Mark Johnson, *Metaphors We Live By*, The University of Chicago Press, Chicago, 1984, ISBN 0-226-46800-3, 242 pp. The authors formulate a controversial theory that all thinking is based on spatial metaphor. Many examples of spatial expressions from everyday speech are provided.

Lockwood, Arthur, *Diagrams*, Watson-Guptill Publications, New York, 1969, British ISBN 289-37030-2, 144 pp. This visual survey of charts, maps, and diagrams for the graphic designer includes some examples of spatial images.

Loran, Erle, *Cézanne's Composition: Analysis of His Form with Diagrams and Photographs of His Motifs*, University of California Press, Berkeley, 1963, 143 pp. The author conducts a detailed proportional and spatial analysis of the painter's work.

March, Lionel, and Philip Steadman, *The Geometry of Environment: An Introduction to Spatial Organization in Design*, RIBA Publications, London, 1971, 360 pp. The authors fuse art and mathematics, as well as architecture and design with modern geometry. Concepts including transformations, symmetry groups, sets, and graphs are also discussed.

Marcus, Aaron "Corporate Identity for Iconic Interface Design: The Graphic Design Perspective," *IEEE Computer Graphics and Applications* 4, no. 7, December 1984, pp. 24ff. The article establishes the concept of corporate or product design integrity, which may be applied to all aspects of user-interface design.

————, et al.,"Screen Design Guidelines," *Proceedings National Computer Graphics Association Annual Conference and Exposition,* 14-18 April 1985, National Computer Graphics Association, Fairfax, VA, 1985, pp. 105-137. Examples of spatial metaphors and spatial objects are briefly presented.

Morgan, Hal, and Dan Symmes, *Amazing 3-D*, Little, Brown, and Co., Boston, 1983, ISBN 0-316-58283-2, 176 pp. The authors review popular culture's fascination with stereoscopic images in the cinema and in comic books.

Piaget, Jean, and Bärbel Inhelder, *The Child's Conception of Space*, W.W. Norton and Co., New York, 1967, ISBN 393-00408-2, 490 pp. This classic work presents Piaget's investigation of how children imagine or visualize spatial entities and spatial characteristics of objects, and how the logical and psychological systems at work are interrelated.

Pevsner, Nikolaus, *An Outline of European Architecture*, Penguin Books, Baltimore, 1963, 496 pp. A noted author explains the development and significance of the architectural form that has predominantly shaped American architectural history.

Stevens, Peter S., *Handbook of Regular Patters: An Introduction to Symmetry in Two Dimensions*, MIT Press, Cambridge, 1981, ISBN 0-262-19188-1, 400 pp. The author explains, with examples, many spatial patterns used in architectural, ornamental, religious, and commercial forms across cultures and through history.

Thomas, Richard K., *Three-Dimensional Design: A Cellular Approach*, Van Nostrand Reinhold Co., New York, 1969, ISBN 0-442-313488-9, 96 pp. The author proposes a three-dimensional design approach emphasizing cells as units of structure and functional space.

Thompson, D'Arcy, *On Growth and Form*, ed. J.T. Bonner, Cambridge University Press, Cambridge, 1966, 346 pp. This classic work discusses the way natural forms grow and the shapes they take.

Weyl, Hermann, *Symmetry*, Princeton University Press, Princeton, 1966, 168 pp. A noted mathematician and philosopher explains the concept of symmetry, beginning with the notion of symmetry as a harmony of proportions.

Conclusion

The availability of relatively inexpensive spatial-imagery systems coincides with an increasing need for effective spatial display and spatial objects by marketing and research/development staffs. The general public also has a need for and interest in spatial imagery. Improvements in the means for communicating spatial facts, concepts, and emotions to inform, persuade, and aesthetically please the reader/viewer is a major challenge for contemporary design of user interfaces and information graphics.

The list of publications provides a starting point for analysis, planning, design, and production of spatial displays and spatial-interaction devices. The references presented here have been chosen because they present their content well both in a verbal and visual form, and because most of them are available in art and design bookstores or from distributors. Equipped with the background that these publications provide, programmers, managers, writers, editors, secretaries, and researchers, that is all those suddenly involved with developing and using spatial user interfaces and spatial information graphics on CRTs, on slide screens, and in publications, can make better decisions about designing spatial imagery and produce higher visual quality in terms of communication effectiveness.

Chapter 2   **Typography**

Even the most advanced graphical display relies on prose text, lists, tables, and forms to convey information. In addition, complex charts, maps, and diagrams use typographic annotation to adequately display their contents. The careful selection of typefaces, fonts, type sizes, and typesetting techniques is a basic requirement for effective design of pages, slides, and screens.

Much research in legibility and readability for text display is available in graphic design and human factors references. This chapter summarizes several basic principles related to topics such as line length, capitalization, etc.

2.1 Making Type Decisions

Introduction

Graphics technology in hardcopy and screen display uses increasingly sophisticated font depiction. Builders and users of these systems need to recognize some of the basic issues of legibility and readability in achieving good design.

Most of us who use word processing and graphics display systems take advantage of this high-level technology to read, write, and draw quickly and efficiently. The letters we read and write are usually no longer the product of our manual dexterity, and we tend to take our alphabet for granted. An interesting change is occurring in technology: display systems are no longer allowing us to ignore type and typography. As printer, plotter, and screen technologies continue to advance, almost every developer and user of graphics display systems is required to make some decisions about the typographic appearance of graphics, even if it is nothing more than whether the title should or should not be centered on a chart.

Type and typography is a subject with a long and complex history that encompasses the evolution of writing systems. The letters and numbers we use are forms that have resulted from thousands of years of evolution. In fact, writing consists of 4 systems of marks that have merged into one visible language system: capital letters, lowercase letters, numbers, punctuation, and other miscellaneous symbols.

Our capital letters derive essentially from Roman letter forms carved into stone. These letter shapes matured approximately 2000 years ago, and they introduced variations in letter widths and stroke widths as well as serifs (small terminating marks at the end of letter strokes). The lowercase letters derive from pen and ink characters intended for parchment. These mutations of the original Roman forms changed over centuries until Charlemagne and Alcuin of York standardized a version during the time of the Holy Roman Empire. Our numerals are Hindu-Arabic in origin and derive from marks invented approximately at the same time in those Asian and Middle Eastern lands: they achieved widespread use in Europe only after gradually supplanting Roman numerals about 700 years ago. Punctuation marks have evolved since the earliest Roman times when little or no punctuation was used to distinguish sentences. Our use of capital letters with lowercase letters derives from the Humanist scholars of the Italian Renaissance who cherished early Roman letter forms and chose to combine them with then current alphabet letters. Historically, culturally, and aesthetically different symbols merged in the typesetting and printing invention of Gutenberg. It is no wonder that good typography requires careful planning and sensitivity to the different factors of form and functionality.

Typefaces

During the past 500 years the basic shapes of our letter forms have not changed greatly; however, typographers have designed many different styles of letter forms that are grouped into several broad categories. The terminology is varied, but one useful set is given in Fig. 2.1 with representative typefaces shown in Fig. 2.2. Those typefaces shown in Fig. 2.2 have demonstrated their durability, appeal, and practicality over many decades and in some cases, centuries. Figure 2.3 identifies many of the important visual characteristics of typographic appearance.

In some cases, typefaces that normally appear on textbook pages today have seen regular use for over 400 years. There are currently several thousand different typefaces available in a variety of display media. Not all of them are used in computer graphics systems. Most are inappropriate for text type because of their limited legibility. As hardcopy and softcopy devices acquire typeface distinctiveness, developer and user groups should demand the most legible and functional typefaces that are available. At the same time, they must make logical selections of typefaces, sizes, weights, layouts, etc. to produce legible, readable communications.

The older typefaces tend to have less distinction between thick and thin strokes. As they become more "modern," the contrast in width often becomes stronger, and the serifs become sharper or more abruptly fastened to the stroke. Although the sans serif (without serif) letterforms have been used since ancient Greek times, they came into widespread use only in this century. San serif typefaces epitomize functional, corporate typography. Typewriter-like fonts with fixed-width characters are currently in use throughout word processing and most display-screen applications. They often combine characteristics of san serif and square serif letterforms with little or no contrast in stroke width.

Legibility and Readability

Legibility concerns the reader's ability to successfully find, identify, discriminate, and absorb the text readability concerns the ease of interpretation and the text's

Figure 2.1 Typographic Terminology

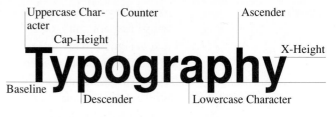

Uppercase Character | Counter | Ascender
Cap-Height | | X-Height
Baseline | Descender | Lowercase Character

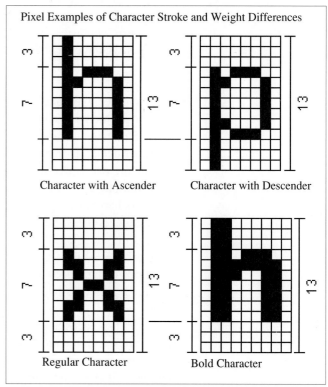

Pixel Examples of Character Stroke and Weight Differences

Character with Ascender   Character with Descender

Regular Character   Bold Character

appeal. Studies have shown that both legibility and readability can be significantly improved through careful selection of type and layout of the material. Although typefaces evolved and page-layout styles changed considerably over the centuries, certain fundamental principles have emerged about which most professionals agree.

Variable-width letters, in which an el, for example, is less wide than an em, consume less space and create more legible texts than fixed-width letters, in which each letter has the same width no matter how simple or complex the letter form. The size of legible letters for

Figure 2.2 Examples
of Typefaces

Univers
This illustration shows
different typographic
styles. Type style is an
important design
consideration and helps
give an overall look to the
document.

Garamond
This illustration shows different
typographic styles. Type style is
an important design consideration
and helps give an overall look to
the document.

Bookman
This illustration shows
different typographic
styles. Type style is an
important design
consideration and helps
give an overall look to the
document.

Helvetica
This illustration shows
different typographic styles.
Type style is an important
design consideration and
helps give an overall look to
the document.

`Courier`
`This illustration`
`shows different`
`typographic styles.`
`Type style is an`
`important design`
`consideration and`
`helps give an overall`
`look to the document.`

Palatino
This illustration shows
different typographic styles.
Type style is an important
design consideration and
helps give an overall look to
the document.

Futura
This illustration shows different
typographic styles. Type style
is an important design
consideration and helps give
an overall look to the
document.

Times
This illustration shows different
typographic styles. Type style is
an important design
consideration and helps give an
overall look to the document.

text varies greatly with individual typeface designs;
legible letters are usually 9 or 10 point sizes (1 point =
1/72 inch). According to Rehe (see Bibliography, Section 2.1), the optimal line length for legible texts is 10
to 12 words per line, or about 18 to 24 picas (1 pica =
1/6 inch = 12 points). In our firm, we usually recommend 40 to 60 characters maximum for line lengths.
This design decision can have a dramatic impact on
layout for 80 or 132 character printers and screens.

One often-asked question is whether serif or sans serif
type is more legible. Studies have shown a slightly

XXXXXXXXXXXXXXXXXXXXX

Line Spacing
Type size plus one to two
points of leading

XXXXXXXXXXXXXXXXXXXX

Word Spacing
1/3 to 1/4 typesize, or
about the width of "r"

word spacing

Line Lengths
40-60 characters

Long lines retard reading, and line lengths of more than 60 characters should be avoided. Unjustified (ragged right) text can usually have better word spacing without gaps between the words.

Paragraphing
Paragraphs should
be separated by
1 blank line space

Long lines retard reading, and line lengths of more than 60 characters should be avoided. Unjustified (ragged right) text can usually have better word spacing without gaps between the words.

Flush Left

Long lines retard reading, and line lengths of more than 60 characters should be avoided. Unjustified (ragged right) text can usually have better word spacing without gaps between the words.

Justified

Long lines retard reading, and line lengths of more than 60 characters should be avoided. Unjustified (ragged right) text can usually have better word spacing without gaps between the words.

Centered

Long lines retard reading, and line lengths of more than 60 characters should be avoided. Unjustified (ragged right) text can usually have better word spacing without gaps between the words.

Figure 2.3 Basic Elements of Typesetting

greater legibility in serif type, but this status can easily be offset by other features of type treatment and layout. Readers often prefer the kind of type that they have had the most experience reading. A typeface selection should be made in relation to the kind of text or document being designed. Bear in mind that san serif typefaces such as Helvetica and Univers have gained wide acceptance as appealing, functional designs for corporate literature, but there is still a tradition that serif type faces are more appropriate for more formal documents. One of the most important considerations for legible typography is any constraint imposed by the previewing or reproduction systems. Obviously, in many low-resolution printer and screen displays, the fine strokes of serifs can not be clearly depicted. In these situations, simple sans serif typefaces of medium weight offer an advantage.

One important characteristic of text areas is the alignment or lack of alignment of the right ends of text lines. Research shows that there is no significant difference in legibility or reader preference between justified (fixed length) and unjustified (flush left, ragged right) lines of type. For many discontinuous texts, for example, those broken up by frequent tables, lists, or examples, unjustified text can help to create a visually more consistent and organized page. Recent human-factors studies show that justified lines of text on CRT screens slows reading speed by 12 percent because of the gaps between words caused by justification of text lines with relatively few characters per line (see Bibliography, Section 2.1, Trollip, 1986).

Another important characteristic of text areas is capitalization. As pointed out by Rehe, words set in all capitals use up 30 percent more space for variable-width letters and retard reading speed by 12 percent. Word shapes are crucial for efficient reading, and capital letters with regular height reduce the variability of word shape presented by lowercase letters with ascenders and descenders. Consequently, uppercase and lowercase settings used together are more legible and readable, making this approach a better choice in typesetting style.

As a general rule for legible text settings, a minimum of differences in typefaces, sizes, and weights should be used. For most text documents, I recommend a maximum of two typefaces (for example, Helvetica and Times Roman), two slants (roman and italic), two weights (medium and bold), and four sizes (main title, subtitle, text, footnote).

Layout

Individual typesetting characteristics must be supported by an overall page or screen layout. As shown in the previous chapter, by establishing a spatial grid in which type elements appear in a consistent location, it is possible to avoid a confusing arrangement of text, tables, and illustrations. For most situations of extensive information retrieval, a clear, regular organization of typography on the page increases legibility and readability. It is possible to arrange symmetric or asymmetric layouts. These proportions should not be mixed within an application. Divide the page or screen into areas of one to three text columns. Be certain to leave space between columns, called gutters, and to account for ample margins around the edges of the visual field. Determine where illustrations will appear and how they will relate to the text columns. Remember to keep the underlying grid simple; variety will emerge from the actual layout of text and illustrations that fill the page or screen.

Conclusion

The use of typeface characteristics, typographic hierarchy (the variations of type weight, typesize, etc.), and spatial composition have been the expertise of the professional graphic designer in the past. Today, with the current variety of display media, lack of standards, variation in quality, and lack of predesigned templates, many users must make their own typographic decisions. This is an added responsibility in creating effective visual communication, but this technological challenge can also lead to the study of typography. To help you find out more about the design of typefaces and designing with type refer to Section 2.1 in the Bibliography. The bibliography provides a selection of references that discuss these issues and principles more thoroughly.

Typography is the key ingredient in text materials and in almost any well-designed table, chart, map, or diagram. We have just scratched the surface of this fascinating subject, and we shall return to this topic in later chapters. In the meantime, start looking at and thinking about the typeface you are now reading!

2.2 Forms Design

Introduction

 Forms are one of the most frequently encountered typographic displays of data or information output. Without the humble form, governments would crumble and the business world would grind to a halt. The flourishing electronic publishing centers within corporations make it more important than ever to give attention to planning, designing, and producing efficient and effective forms as an administrative tool.

In the realm of user-interface design, many complicated applications require a forms-oriented approach for entering data within dialogue boxes, control panels, or entire screens (see Fig. 2.4). Success in forms design involves approaching the problem systematically, analyzing the conceptual content, designing the graphic appearance, designing the verbal content, and evaluating the form.

Good screen layouts follow most of the same principles that standard paper-forms layouts follow. Most screens cannot display small text, but they can allow for dynamic, interactive components, and many can easily display polychromatic elements.

Forms-Design Guidelines

The following recommendations are some general tips for good forms design.

Analyze the contents to determine what titles, labels, and fields belong together.

Too often, older, traditional forms have grown in a chaotic manner with barnacles of information encrusted in them that may not be relevant or useful; in fact, some

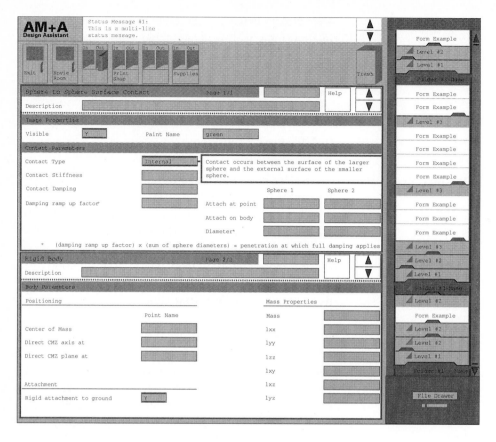

Figure 2.4 An Example
of Forms-Oriented Screen
Layout

of the elements may actually confuse the reader. New forms require scrutiny to determine which elements belong together. It is important to consider systematically who the senders or originators of the form are, what their needs are, who the readers of the form are (both those who fill out the form and those who process the filled-out form), what the readers' needs are, what media used to convey the form are, and what the requirements or limitations of those media are.

For example, senders may not only be reporting information, but may also wish to convey a special sense of authority and competence. Senders might be seeking to encourage recipients to examine unusually complex but important data. If readers are busy, but are expected to return forms, they may have to be encouraged and assisted in special ways. Particular equipment used in preparing forms may have severe limitations in appearance or data manipulation; this, too, will affect the appearance of the form and its use by the reader.

Design the initial layout by creating "bubble diagrams" of the form.

Once you have gathered information and have determined possible contents, create sketches that are, in effect, " bubble diagrams " of the form. These sketches are logical abstractions of the form that indicate probable content elements, their approximate size, and their approximate location. This is a typical stage in the visual design of any complex image. At this stage, it is easier to manipulate broad differences in the form's groupings and hierarchy. It is important not to be too precise or detailed early in the design process. It is more important to explore possible variations. Evaluate which groupings seem to meet the needs of the sender, the receiver, the message, and the medium.

Tell a story visually.

 Sequencing information in the form should follow the natural order for "telling an information story visually" to the reader. This order may be a straightforward movement from top to bottom, but it also may be a complex movement over the surface of the form. Instructions should appear at appropriate and crucial steps in the reading or fill-in process. If instructions begin to appear in too many places and the form begins to appear too cluttered, regroup these instructions in one or two places.

Sort the form into zones.

Spatial grouping of information areas can have a major impact on the perceived complexity of a form. Zones should be established in which all information is grouped by consistent content, purpose, or appearance. It is particularly important to determine an underlying spatial grid to help organize all components within the visual composition, including gray patterns, the extent of ruled lines, etc. The form's overall spatial appearance should immediately correspond to the form's primary content groups and their hierarchy, for example, moving from major to minor zones as the reader goes from the top to the bottom of the form. In general, well-designed forms have a maximum of "seven plus or minus two" major zones that stretch across the entire visual field of the form. This number (called Miller's number in human factors) is a maximum number of major differentiations that the human mind can keep track of in short-term memory.

Design a detailed layout grid that governs all major locations of type, symbols, and images on the form.

Use the grid to establish standard, repetitive, horizontal and/or vertical locations and sizes for all tables, indented lists, field elements, and titling. Avoid any nonstandard tab settings: these settings only confuse the reader's eye roaming the form for instructions and data-field labels, or for data-fields in which to read or enter data.

Forms are primarily complex, spatially structured typography. Let the typography tell the story.

Typographic distinctions should usually be limited to approximately three different sizes of a single family of type (for example, 8, 10, and 20 point Helvetica), with two variations of boldness (medium and bold) or slant (roman and italic) used to provide further distinctions.

Give the form a short, simple, clear, distinctive title.

Anyone glancing at the form should be able to recognize what kind of document it is. The main title should orient the reader immediately to the form's content and purpose. Subtitles should reinforce the conceptual hierarchy and the spatial grouping of areas within the form.

Use large letters, bold titles, ruled lines, or gray areas to separate major zones on the page.

Once a style of separation and annotation is selected, continue to use the same approach as often as possible within the form. Avoid sudden changes in the means of emphasizing or de-emphasizing the importance of certain areas. A typical design style for black-and-white laser-printed forms is the following: use white areas for the fields in which important data or messages appear or for the fields that the reader must fill in. Use black typography on gray for most other areas, such as, labels, instructions, and other annotation. Use large black letters on white for the main title of the form. Use white letters on black bars for the subtitles.

Simplify the alphanumerics.

Coding should be simple and clear. If a form has a major sequence of areas or a general fill-in procedure, number the steps with large numerals so that readers can grasp the necessary sequence easily.

Use legible, readable typographic style.

In general, variable-width, high-quality, and uppercase and lowercase typography should be used for maximum legibility of titles, headings, verbal elements, footnotes, and captions. Especially for prose texts in instructions, all capital settings in forms can slow reading speed by 12 percent.

Keep lines of text short, legible, and readable.

Generally, lines of text should be 40 to 60 characters long for maximum legibility. Appropriate line spacing will depend on the particular typographic fonts used. Flush left, ragged right typography is most suitable for extended prose, for example, instructions, because most of the typography of the form will be interrupted and scattered elements of text.

Use rules and graphic symbolism sparingly.

Rules and large symbols or even illustrational elements can help emphasize important areas within the form and can lead the reader's eye horizontally, vertically, or in any particular path across the page. As with typography, variations in rule lengths and thicknesses, as well as symbol sizes and shapes, should be kept to a minimum, usually three different weights. Use a standard hierarchy for the rules, that is, use the heaviest to differentiate major zones in the form. Note that very thin lines (so-called hairline rules) can be used for the thinnest rules. Too many thick rules in both horizontal and vertical directions make the visual composition too cluttered and distracting. In general, a well-designed form often has a strong, consistent dominance of either vertical or horizontal lines over the entire form, even if it has several zones. Avoid using constantly varying lengths of lines for rules where the captions or labels of the elements to be filled in vary in length. Design the form so that rules can set up a regular visual rhythm even if the captions are irregular in length.

Use color with discretion; too much variation will confuse the reader.

In general, it is reasonable to use one color for most typography and one color for highlighting one class of special titles, data items, labels, or instructions. Gray (shaded) patterns can often be used effectively to lowlight areas that do not need to be filled in or examined carefully. Thin horizontal areas of gray alternating with unshaded areas in numerical tables, for example, can often help make repetitive lines of digits more readable.

Provide sufficient space for handwritten fill-ins.

For forms that must be filled-in manually by the reader, three lines vertically per inch and five digits horizontally per inch account for most typewriters and handwritten entries. Boxed areas within the form should be kept to a minimum, and the boxes should correspond to the overall spatial grid.

Edit the verbal contents to fit the visual design of the form.

The verbal contents of titles, column labels, row labels, instructions, headings, and footnotes should fit the visual basis of the form. It may be necessary to select terminology that has three standard lengths: normal (more than 20 characters), abbreviated (10 to 20 characters), and short (5 to 7 characters). Scrutinize all words, phrases, sentences, and paragraphs for consistency, clarity and succinctness. In general, verbal content should be terse, specific, unambiguous, familiar, and in the active voice. For forms that have been used for a considerable time, it is often necessary to discuss with the senders possible changes in terminology. The staff may no longer know why the terminology was chosen. Make the terminology as brief, appropriate, and effective as it can be.

Tables should have a consistent design.

Use right-adjusted entries for numerical lists. Numerical lists with decimal values usually should align the decimal points. Use flush left entries for alphabetic lists, which makes it easier for the eye to scan vertically for unfamiliar or familiar words or letter combinations. Avoid centered lists because they are harder to scan. Even the column labels should relate to the contents of the lists, that is, they should be flush left or flush right depending on the contents below them.

If in doubt, do it consistently.

In general, use a consistent approach for everything, unless there is a specific need to differentiate lengths, typefaces, weights, spacing, etc. The visual differences in a form should be as meaningful as possible from a communication perspective; otherwise, the random or idiosyncratic changes merely add more processing time for the human mind and create the possibility of misinterpretation.

Evaluate your designs by showing them to potential readers.

Prototypes should be circulated immediately among managers, technical staff, senders, and typical receivers for their review. Their evaluation can affect the conceptual, visual, and verbal content of the form. This cycle should be repeated one or more times, depending upon schedule deadlines. The form designer must constantly search for inconsistencies that could confuse the reader.

Conclusion

While no set of rules can guarantee a perfectly designed form, the techniques and principles described in this section can guide the designer to improved forms design. Bibliography, Section 2.2 provides some additional information for those who would like to pursue the subject more thoroughly.

2.3 The Typography of Complex Documentation: Computer Programs

Introduction

Besides Bibles and telephone books, one of the largest worldwide publishing efforts is the documentation of computer programs. Surprisingly, this activity receives relatively little attention from the general public or even from the computer-technology community responsible for writing, editing, publishing, and distributing these documents. Programs are a new form of literature, with its own languages, styles of writing, devoted audiences, and emotional debates about what constitutes good program writing. Good programs are concerned with structure and content, as well as appearance and form. As the visually oriented poets have been saying in the twentieth century since Apollinaire wrote *Calligrammes* (Bibliography, Section 2.3), the appearance of a given text can be as important as its content. Researchers have proved this theory. The journal *Visible Language* (Bibliography, Section 2.3, Wendt 1979) reports giving readers a choice of plain text, text highlighted with good typography and a few illustrations, or a highly visual text with many illustrations. Results showed that the readers' rate of comprehension increased with the latter two choices, and that most readers preferred the highly visual layout.

This survey points out the importance of both legibility and readability. Because the readers are human beings and not machines, both factors are important, especially to computer program literature, which is dense, complex, and sometimes read by captive readers who are not at all happy to be reading it under current circumstances of documentation.

The appearance of programs has been virtually unchanged since the beginning of programming, yet the technology of text presentation (and illustration) has dramatically changed. Today, specialized document-preparation equipment for electronic publishing, such as the workstations with Interleaf, Intergraph, or Context software, and even the ubiquitous Apple Macintosh with the LaserWriter, can easily prepare documents with a variety of typefaces and sophisticated layouts. This equipment can be used to enhance the appearance of computer programs to make them more legible, readable, comprehensible, memorable, and maintainable. With writing programs generally costing at least 50 dollars per line of code, any improvements in the efficiency with which programs are written and maintained can easily translate to significant cost savings.

Research in Program Visualization The notion of improved program appearance began with pretty printing programs that made some attempts to group characters more judiciously and accomplished minor cleanup of out-of-control line printers. A more serious effort was undertaken by the U.S. Defense Department's Advanced Research Projects Agency (DARPA), which sponsored three years of research in program visualization by our firm and Professor Ron Baecker, Computer Science Department, University of Toronto, then president of Human Computing Resources, Toronto. The work accomplished for this project is outlined here as an illustration of what the programming community can expect in the next few years as program documentation matures with other areas of electronic publishing. The project is described in detail in *Human Factors and Typography for More Readable Programs,* by Baecker and Marcus (see Bibliography, Section 2.3).

One goal of the project was to produce a " visual C compiler " that would be able to interpret an ordinary C program and automatically redesign the program's appearance as the computer was also coming to understand it. The program documentation would be enhanced for presentation by laser printer or phototypesetter technology. The approach used the principles of systems- and information-oriented graphic design to develop new representations of program source code that used multiple fonts, variable point sizes, variable character widths, proportional character spacing, variable word and line spacing, nonalphanumeric symbols, gray scale tints, rules, and arbitrary spatial location of elements on a page.

Folk Designs and Prototypes

Before prototypes were developed, the research team examined conventional, or "folk designs," for program source code. Using Intran's Metaform software and a QMS laser printer, myself and my graphic design staff developed prototypes that were reviewed by Ron Baecker and his computer science colleagues. The latter group developed versions of a code compiler/typesetter that brought the output closer and closer to the optimum visual solution.

In-house programming staff and computing professionals, in addition to the graphic design staff, critiqued the prototypes. The research effort accomplished the following: our firm, with the assistance of Human Computing Resources, prepared a graphic design manual for the appearance of C source code. Human Computing Resources, with the assistance of our firm, wrote code for a compiler with over 100 different parameters that can be varied individually to "tune" the appearance of the code.

Design Principles

The conventions for the appearance of code evolved through a series of experiments that produced the following design principles. These design principles apply to all complex documentation. Examples of a typical program and an enhanced version of program depiction are shown in Figs. 2.5, 2.6, and 2.7.

Typographic Vocabulary: It is wise to choose a small number of type styles of suitable legibility, clarity, and distinguishability and apply them thoughtfully to encode and distinguish various kinds of program elements or tokens. Within each typeface, it is necessary to choose or design a set of special letterforms and symbols to represent the text effectively.

For the improvements shown in Figs. 2.6 and 2.7, Helvetica and Times Roman are used to distinguish between source code itself and comments or commentary that appear to help the reader understand the meaning of the code. These two typefaces are used in bold roman, regular roman, and regular italic variations. For example, most of the code appears in regular sans serif Helvetica, while reserved words are shown in italic sans serif type. Bold sans serif is used to highlight global variables.

Typesetting Parameters: It is necessary to adjust the text point size, headline size and usage, word spacing, paragraph indentation, and line spacing to accommodate source code. Standard text sizes are used for the presentation of code, while smaller sizes are used for supplementary information. Special changes have been made to optimize the reading of C. For example, the visual C compiler automatically makes word spacing adjustments around phrases of code to help the reader's eye group the line into its proper components. In addition, parentheses and brackets are made bold to catch the reader's attention to grouped items.

Page Composition: By carefully controlling the 8.5 x 11 inch page's composition through the use of a specific layout grid, the program's structure can be made

Figure 2.5 A Portion of a
Typical C Program

```
Apr 20 12:54 1989  phone.c Page 1


/*
 * phone.c - Prints all potential words corresponding to a given phone number.
 *
 * Only words containing vowels are printed.
 * Acceptable phone numbers range from 1 to 10 digits.
 */

#include <string.h>
#include <stdio.h>

typedef int     bool;
#define FALSE   0
#define TRUE    1

char    *label[] = { /* labels on each digit of dial */
    "0",
    "1",            "abc",  "def",
    "ghi",          "jkl",  "mno",
    "prs",          "tuv",  "wxy"
};

#define PNMAX   10      /* max digits in phone number */

int     digits; /* actual number of digits */
int     pn[PNMAX];          /* phone number */
char    *label_ptr[PNMAX];      /* current position in label, per digit */

main(argc, argv)
    int argc;
    char        *argv[];
{
    register int        i;
    bool        foundvowel = FALSE;

    /* For each phone argument ... */
    while (*++argv != NULL) {
        if (!getpn(*argv))
            fprintf(stderr, "PhoneName:  %s is not a phone number\n", *argv);
        else {
            /* For beginnings of label sequences */
            for (i = 0; i < PNMAX; ++i)  /* Reset label_ptr (pointers).*/
                label_ptr[i] = label[pn[i]];
            /* For each combination of characters ... */
            do {
                for (i = 0; i < digits; ++i) {
                    if (strchr("aeiou", *label_ptr[i]) != NULL)
                        foundvowel = TRUE;
                }
                if (foundvowel)  /* Only print things with vowels! */
                {
                    for (i=0; i!=digits; i++)
                        printf("%c",*label_ptr[i]);
                    printf("\n");
                }
                foundvowel = FALSE;
            } while (incr());
```

more apparent. Typographic rules can also be used to help reinforce the visual rhythm of the grid.

The page is divided into a main column 31 picas wide (about 5 inches) for code and a secondary column to the left 11 picas wide (about 2 inches) for marginalia, that is, one-line commentary on the code. As code steps deeper and deeper into subactivities, the text tabs over to the right, so that the readers are always able to sense the level at which they are reading. In this manner, even "empty" white space has significance within the page layout. Indentations make the standard symbols of C program grouping, the brackets, unnecessary. Systematic indentation and placement of key statements occurs for such statements as the *if, do.while,* and *switch* statements.

Figure 2.6 A Portion of
a Prototype Redesigned
Program

Figure 2.7 An Enlarged
Area of Program Text

Symbols and Diagrammatic Elements: Special additional symbols, diagrammatic elements, and graphic forms must be integrated into the depiction to make essential program structure more apparent and appealing. Large brackets and other devices help guide the reader's eye. These supplementary graphic signs are examples of visual, nontextual enhancements to the source code.

Metatext: Beyond the source code itself, additional supplementary text can help the reader interpret and gain perspective. For example, the header and footer of each page contain important information that can guide the reader. The header contains, among other things, the name of the program, the file being listed, the date and time the file was last changed, and three levels of titles that help readers understand where in the text they are reading. The footer contains references to other locations in the text where particular variables are defined and used; in effect, a cross-referenced index is distributed in footnotes throughout the program. Traditional comments appear in the main column.

Conclusion

Many interesting areas for further study emerged from this research. A discovered limitation is that there is, as yet, no typeface designed specifically for code presentation, which places a greater emphasis on punctuation and numbers than normal prose text. This approach needs to be extended to other languages, to color presentations, and of course to screen display, not only paper documentation. Nevertheless, this prototype achievement points the way to the advantages of effective graphic design of computer programs themselves.

As the electronic publishing industry continues to develop, many of these issues will be addressed. Like the proverbial shoemaker's children, programmers are among the last to receive the benefits of computer graphics. The effective visualization of programs themselves promises to beautify and make more productive the daily experience of the people who make the computer graphics world possible.

Chapter 3   Symbolism

Signs, symbols, icons, cursors, and other specialized graphics are popular in paper documents, audio-visual presentations, and user interfaces. These graphics provide functional guidance, aesthetic charm, and corporate or product identity. In the past decade, developers gave relatively little attention to research, analysis, design, and evaluation of this component of visible language. Today, however, products often employ hundreds and even thousands of icons. The current decade will provide increasing commercial, cultural, technological, political, and educational incentives to make these pictographic and ideographic elements work well as a system of signs.

3.1 Clarity and Consistency in Icon Design

Introduction

Nonverbal pictograms, glyphs, and symbols are finding their way into more workstations for office automation, CAD, CAM, CAE, computer-aided education and training, art and design, and even programming. These signs are used to represent options for actions, cursors locating points on the screen, and other structures or processes. People building and using these computer graphics systems often ask three questions: What exactly are icons and symbols? How can we best use them? What should they look like? This section attempts to answer these questions.

Visual Semiotics

One of the first matters that needs clarification is the terminology. What exactly is an icon? If we turn to the discipline of semiotics, the science of signs and their meaning, we will learn that there are three kinds of signs: icon, index, and symbol.

An icon is something that looks like what it means: it is representational and easy to understand. An example is a line of ink standing for a geometric line in a textbook illustration. An index is a sign that was "caused" by the thing or process to which it refers. The trail of muddy footsteps in a front hallway is an index that the children have just entered. A symbol is a sign that may be completely arbitrary in appearance. We often must learn to make the association between a symbol and its meaning, and we must agree that such a symbol will mean a certain thing. An example is the American flag standing for the United States. As you may already realize, all of the letters you are now reading are symbols, the kind called phonograms. Because sounds are not visible to the eye, their appearance as letters in our phonetic alphabet is a matter of historical convention.

Strictly speaking, the so-called icons in iconic interfaces are a mixture of icons, indexes, and symbols. The spread of advertisements and literature about the Xerox Star, the Apple Lisa, and the more recent Apple Macintosh established the term "icon" in the lexicon of computer graphics during the 1980s. Here, I refer to these graphic forms loosely as icons, symbols, or generally as signs. There are four other, more technical terms from semiotics to keep in mind. These terms concern what signs mean: lexical qualities, syntactics, semantics, and pragmatics. In the next section we shall look at design issues for each of these four terms.

Lexical qualities concern how signs are produced. For example, what kinds of marks can a CRT device make? Do they appear as picture elements called pixels or as straight line segments called vectors? Each kind of visible mark influences the kind of signs that can be displayed.

Syntactics refers to the sign's appearance: are they circular, red, big, on the left, or moving? Such features of their appearance can be significant and can communicate a relationship that is important for a class of signs. For example, square icons of a single size can be easily assembled into an efficient, space-filling, regular pattern on the screen.

Semantics is often understood to be the meaning of the term "meaning": to what do these signs refer? These signs can stand for physical objects, people, actions, ideas, or sounds. A sign, for example, may denote the action of exiting from the system or deleting an object called a file.

Pragmatics concerns how signs are consumed. We may ask: will the CRT refresh rate cause disturbing flicker? Can a viewer 28 inches from the screen identify the sign? Part of a sign's total meaning or significance lies in the answers to such questions.

Advantages and Disadvantages

Why are icons and symbols becoming so popular in computer graphics systems? What advantages do they offer over words? Part of the answer lies in the realm of marketing: icons can be entertaining, clever, and visually appealing. Another advantage is that an individual sign may take up fewer pixels and less space than the equivalent in words. Therefore, more information can be packed into a given window or screen space. The space savings in menus, maps, and diagrams can be significant. Even more important, icons and symbols can replace written languages and contribute to interfaces that are international in design and comprehension.

If the signs are well conceived, systematically designed, and effectively displayed, the icons and symbols should be easier to recognize quickly than their verbal counterparts in a busy visual context. Within a window filled by text, for example, a short phrase at the bottom of the window might explain that more text could be displayed if the user scrolls the window contents. This information could be symbolized with a simple arrow that effectively communicates the message and clearly distinguishes itself from alphanumeric text material.

Another primary advantage is the value of icons and symbols in reinforcing and aiding user comprehension of previously delivered verbal information. In tutorial and training materials, for example, a simple question mark inside a round circle can efficiently denote a source of help for the user or a source of confusion for the computer that the computer is bringing to the attention of the user. With just a few pixels, an entire situation and course of action can be implied.

However, icons and symbols are not a panacea for electronic publishing or user-interface design; they can not completely replace words in some complex situations. There are clear disadvantages to the use of icons and symbols. An entire repertoire of new icons must be researched, designed, tested, and introduced into the marketplace. There is no system in existence that may be readily incorporated, unlike letterforms and typefonts. Some international sign languages like Blissymbolics and Ota's LoCos (see Bibliography, Section 3.1) provide a starting point, but these new visible languages must be replanned and redesigned. This is a costly and time-consuming task if it is done well; the consequences of poor design are confusion and lower productivity for the user. As with typefaces, the signs often must appear in different sizes, weights, and styles. An entire "font" of symbols would have to be designed for each major size.

There are some examples of designing graphic symbol well in other fields. For example, the U.S. Department of Transportation commissioned a study that made recommendations for the use of symbols in mass-transit environments (see Bibliography, Section 3.1, Symbol Signs). Skilled graphic designers created conventions for symbols that have improved the quality of such signage throughout the country. Similar activities are necessary in the computer graphics field where signage systems for the mind are now being built into user interfaces.

Because of difficulties in designing, teaching, and comprehending icons and symbols, there is a practical limit to how many different local and global signs can be introduced into a system. Even the pictographic/ideographic Chinese system, with its large repertoire of signs, has a much smaller number of signs (approximately 3000) that most people use in practice. Ideally, icons and symbols should be used for what they can do best, to communicate concepts effectively within a small area of space. At the same time they should retain a clear, consistent approach. This leads us to consider some of the graphic design issues.

Design Issues

Basic principles for designing systems of icons and symbols are similar to those for designing the larger-scale windows and screens. Consistency, clarity, simplicity, and familiarity are key attributes. Sometimes these factors will be at cross purposes, but this is not unusual in design tasks. The skilled professional knows when to weigh one factor more heavily than another. Let us look at a few typical symbols exhibiting these properties.

Figure 3.1 shows a set of signs that demonstrate how graphic design consistency can be established among icons and symbols. The grid indicates the number of pixels used to display the icon. The pixels must be of sufficient quantity and size to establish clear differences of form so that the icons can be identified by the user at normal viewing distance. On high-resolution screens (60 to 150 dots per inch), 30 to 60 pixels are

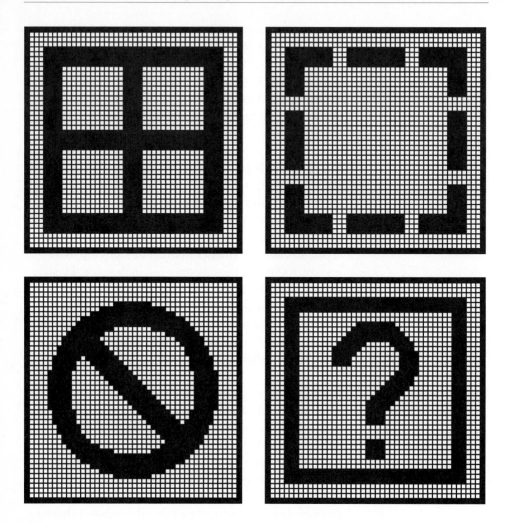

Figure 3.1 Signs Developed
for Perq Accent Operating
System

often used. Keep in mind that industy standard CGA, EGA, and VGA screen resolutions are all different, including differently shaped pixels. Icons must be designed to appear correctly in each of these screen display standards.

The prototypes in Fig. 3.1 demonstrate how typical graphical editing concepts might be shown. Each symbol uses a set of visual elements in different ways to build up an image. This process guarantees a modicum of syntactic consistency and also allows the symbols to be easily distinguished. The designer can establish icon

Figure 3.2 Icons Developed
for Intran Metaform
Workstation

Conclusion

and symbol consistency through limiting the variations
of angles, line thicknesses, shapes, amount of empty
space, etc.

Figure 3.2 shows icons from the Intran Metaform system, one of the earlier iconic user interfaces that appeared in 1983, about one month before the Apple Lisa.
In comparison to the typical icons of the Apple
Macintosh, the Metaform icons are very elaborate illustrations describing the typical activities within the module. They resemble illuminated letters from medieval
manuscripts and clarify what is happening in a particular module. Our firm designed these prototypes for
clerical staff who operated the equipment and were unfamiliar with computer technology. The signs are intended to intrigue and appeal to this user group.

Figure 3.3 shows how the style of symbol drawing can
be varied to present a corporate-identity approach to
depicting the basic shape or form. Care must be taken
to ensure that such manipulations do not adversely affect legibility.

Figure 3.4 shows how complex even simple symbols
can become. One symbol from Perq's Accent operating
system, which our firm also designed, shows an icon
with a subicon inside of it. These variations of signs
show how using a simple set of sign parts can help
communicate many different pieces of information.

We are seeing an evolution of writing systems in
computer-based visual communication. Some companies are beginning to devote significant time to the
graphic design of these new icons and symbols. We
have already mentioned the pioneering work of
developers at Xerox and at Apple. Dicomed, another
manufacturer of CRT display equipment, spent considerable time in the 1980s improving the icons and
symbols of workstations intended for graphic artists
and designers. Interleaf's document layout system

Figure 3.3 Corporate
Identity Reflected in an
Icon Set

introduced in the 1980s also showed sophisticated, comprehensible approach to icons and symbols.

More investigation needs to be done in this important area. The design and use of icons and symbols can be expected to increase for most popular computing and for many specialized professional workstations. Bibliography Sections 3.1, 3.2, and 3.3 will help readers recognize the elements that contribute to the design of effective symbols and icons for electronic publishing and user-interface design.

3.2 Icon Design Tips

Introduction

Icons, symbols, pictograms, ideograms, and other signs are quickly becoming indispensable as components of user interfaces in successful computer graphics products. In recent years, icons have become more colorful, dynamic, acoustic (that is, accompanied by voice or music elements), three-dimensional in appearance, and certainly more ubiquitous. In fact, it is not uncommon for CAD/CAM/CAE systems to employ thousands of these small images to help convey choices of functions, data, tool kits, window-manipulation markers, or navigation devices. Successful icon design involves approaching the problem systematically, analyzing the sometimes conflicting needs that determine appearance and interaction characteristics, designing prototypes, and evaluating the designs.

Figure 3.4 Four Complex
Ideograms Assembled from
Iconic Components

In Section 3.4, a reading list is provided on icon design.
One of the best references cited Ota's *Pictogram
Design* (see also Bibliography, Section 3.2 and 3.4).
This profusely illustrated, bilingual (Japanese and
English) work provides an historical overview, with ex-
amples in color, and many excellent case studies of
icon and symbol design.

Icon Design Issues
Lexical Issues:
How are signs
produced?

The following is an initial list of issues that the icon designer faces. The list is based on the terminology of semiotics.

What spatial resolutions are available?

What size limits (minimum and maximum) exist?

What duration and frequency of change (animation) attributes exist?

What brightness levels and colors are available?

What acoustic attributes exist?

What shading, corner, angle, line thickness, and other appearance attributes are available?

Syntactic Issues:
How do the signs
appear in space
and time?

What are the systematic, regular conditions of these attributes:

Size, shape
Line thickness, line pattern, line terminations
Patterns
Orientation
Location
Color
Animation
Spatial grids
Modular parts

Semantic Issues:
To what do the
signs refer?

What are the systematic references of the signs?

Concrete objects
Abstract objects
Part of referent versus whole referent
Moment in time (before/during/after event)

Pragmatic Issues:
How are the signs
used?

Are the icons legible under typical viewing distances
and ambient lighting?

Can the icons be identified easily both individually and
within groups?

Can the icons be remembered easily?

Do the numbers and kinds of shapes, patterns, or colors
create confusion?

Are the icons pleasing to the eye?

**Icon Design
Guidelines**

As for forms, the following recommendations are some
general tips for good icon design.

Analyze the verbal contents and the display environment.

Determine how icon parts and complete icons should
relate. Existing icons have developed in an often chaotic manner with elements that may not be relevant, consistent, or useful. Too many parts may confuse the
viewer. The icon-display equipment may have severe
limitations in appearance or interaction characteristics
(for example, monochrome CRTs or touch-screen input), which will affect the appearance of the icons and
their use by the viewer.

Design the initial icons by creating quick sketches.

Once the semantic contents has been organized, create
many quick sketches that may vary from logical abstractions to concrete images. Indicate all visual elements, their approximate size, and their approximate
location. This is a typical stage in the visual design of a
complex system of images. At this stage it is easier to
manipulate broad differences in the icons and their hierarchy. It is important not to be too precise or detailed
early in the design process. It is more important to

Figure 3.5 Grid-Based
Symbol Signs

explore possible variations. Evaluate which icons seem to meet the needs of the sender, the receiver, the message, and the medium.

Sort the icons into styles.

Consistent stylistic treatment has a major effect on the perceived complexity of the icons. Styles should be established in which all the icons are grouped by consistent approach (for example, part for a whole) or appearance (for example, curved versus angular shapes). By sorting the sketches, it is easier to keep track of trade-offs in optimizing the entire set of icons with regard to simplicity, clarity, and consistency.

Design a layout grid that organizes all major elements of the icons.

Determine an underlying spatial grid (see Fig. 3.5) to make consistent all visual components, including point elements, gray patterns, curves, angles, the length and width of rules, etc. It is especially important to use the grid to establish standard horizontal, vertical, and oblique lines and a limited set of sizes for objects.

Use large objects, bold lines, and simple areas to distinguish icons.

Once a style of presentation is selected, continue to use the same approach as often as possible within the icon set. Avoid sudden changes in the means of emphasizing or de-emphasizing the importance of certain objects, structures, or processes. Avoid making crucial elements of the icon's significance too small in comparison to the total size of the icon.

Simplify appearance.

Icons should be simple and clear. Any extraneous decorative parts should be carefully weighed against the confusion they may cause the viewer. On the other hand, the icons should not be so simple that they all seem identical; they should be clearly distinguishable. The visual differences in an icon should be as significant as possible from a communication perspective; otherwise, the random or idiosyncratic changes merely add more processing time for the human mind and create a possibility of errors of interpretation.

Use color with discretion.

Too much variation will confuse the viewer with distracting clutter. In general, for color displays it is reasonable to use five or fewer colors (including black, white, and/or gray) for icons. Simple color patterns often can be used effectively for background or lowlighted areas that do not need to be examined carefully.

Evaluate the designs by showing them to potential viewers.

After prototypes are available, these should be reviewed and tested by typical viewers. Green and Burgess' report (see Bibliography, Section 3.2) explains how to set up an evaluation. Evaluations, which can affect all aspects of icon design, should be repeated if resources and project deadlines permit.

Icon Design Trends   Icon design has entered a new phase in recent years. In May 1988, Xerox was awarded U.S. design patents for icons such as file folder, wastebasket, floppy disk drive, and telephone (see Fig. 3.6). Design patents, which protect the aesthetic appearance of "ornamental" designs, have been granted in other areas of the design professions, but these are some of the first to be awarded in computer graphics.

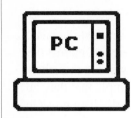

Patent number 295,633
Icon for PC Emulation or the Like
Doris E. Wells-Papanek; William L. Verplank, both of
Menlo Park, and Norman L. Cox, Mountain View, all of
Calif., assignors to Xerox Corporation, Stamford, Conn.
Filed Oct. 28, 1985, Ser. No. 791,852
Term of patent 14 years, U.S. Cl. D18-27

Figure 3.6 Recently
Patented Icon Designs

Kluth and Lundberg's article (see Bibliography,
Section 3.2) discusses in detail the proprietary rights
for this new form of intellectual property. Designers,
lawyers, manufacturers, and consumers will be interested in these developments. At the same time, standards
organizations, such as the International Standards
Organization (ISO) and the American National
Standards Institute (ANSI), have made efforts to establish icon standards for various disciplines and classes
of equipment.

Conclusion

Does this mean an end to creativity in icon design?
Hardly: the need for well-designed icons will continue
unabated. The seriousness of the discipline; the time,
effort, and resources good icon design requires; and the
commercial and legal implications of the designs,
however, will all acquire maturity in the next several
years. No set of rules can guarantee a perfectly
designed icon, but the techniques and principles
discussed should help.

3.3 Icon Design in a CAD/CAM
Graphical User Interface: A Case Study

Introduction

Over the past several decades, CAE/CAD/CAM have
become widely used as a key component of computer-
integrated manufacturing (CIM). As the complexity of
these systems has increased dramatically, the user
community has evolved to include many nontechnical

staff members for whom even basic CAD/CAM functions may appear confusing. These opposing factors place increasing pressure on manufacturers to improve the ease of learning and using CAD/CAM systems.

One approach to upgrading CAD/CAM user interfaces is to enhance the visible language presentation of the screens: the typography, symbolism, color, layout, and sequencing of all command-control and documentation content. The general design goals are to improve the legibility and readability of screens and to increase simplicity, clarity, and consistency of all functions and data. Other chapters of this book concern various facets of user-interface design. This section will focus on selected aspects of the redesign of the screens for a particular product, the Computervision (now part of Prime Computer) CADD Station.

Several vendors offer CAD/CAM products with a wide range of functionality, medium- or high-resolution screen display, and icon-oriented user interfaces. Computervision's solution is one of the more highly integrated approaches, and the user-interface design issues described here should be instructive to all those professionals engaged in advanced graphical user-interface design.

A CAE/CAD/CAM Configuration   At the time of the design project in the late 1980s, the Computervision CAE/CAD/CAM software ran under the UNIX operating system and the Sun-based Network File System. The workstation included functionality for schematic capture, logic simulation, printed circuit-board layout, numerical control, plant design, mapping, and other modules.

The Sun hardware featured a 19-inch landscape monochrome or color monitor with an image area of 1152 horizontal by 900 vertical square pixels, or 81 pixels per inch. The SunView interface provided for up to 16 simultaneous overlapping or tiled windows via the Suntools package. The user interface allowed users to work on and view four simultaneous, independent tasks as well as to access the UNIX shell and Sun desktop applications by providing screen space for Sun icon-based commands.

As shown in Fig. 3.7 the Computervision CADDS user interface consists of four primary windows:

Graphics window
Status window
Text window
Menu window

A typical screen layout of the user interface shows the design of subassemblies and their components. A status window across the top above the graphics window does not appear in this particular view. Note the global commands at the upper-right of the menu, the local commands below them, the alphanumeric keypad, and the "local global" commands at the lower-right of the menu. The global icons appear without a border and therefore have varying degrees of "tightness of fit." Note the small symbol of the turned-up page corner in the lower-right local command. This sign reference is an example of icon-class symbolism that makes the area for the nonverbal symbol of the icon more cluttered.

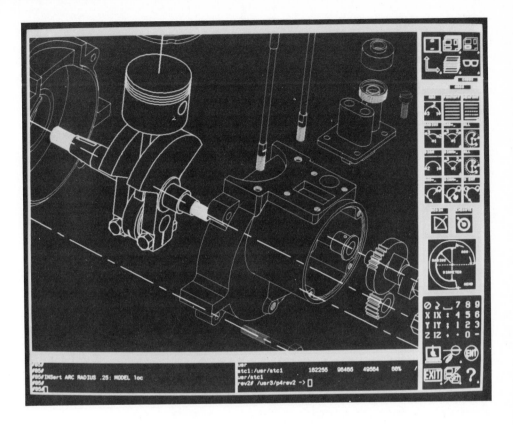

Figure 3.7
Computervision's
User Interface

The performance of sophisticated CAD/CAM tasks was carried out by selecting from icon groups in the menu area. These functions included global operations accessible throughout the user interface at the top of the screen. For some operations, after selecting an icon for the operation, a pulldown menu would appear to help select the particular command needed. For other operations, further groups of icons appeared to aid operation selection.

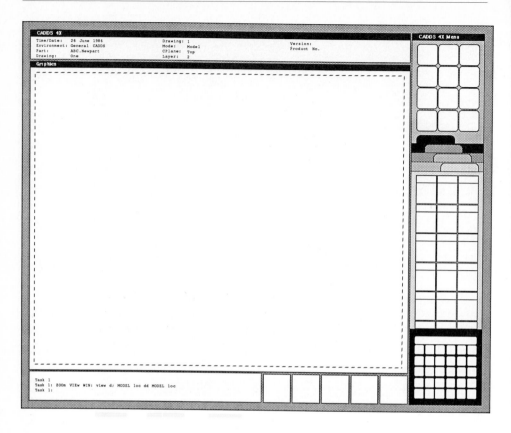

Figure 3.8 A Typical Screen Layout of the Revised CADD Station Screen

The dotted line indicates the image display area.

The functional modules for the product were built over many months by staff in several locations. In this medium- to high-resolution screen environment, there were many possible ways for icons and details of screen display to appear. With many people working to design an effective user interface, there was a consequent need for guidelines and detailed specifications.

The User-Interface Manual: Icon Design

Computervision recognized that the complexity of visual appearance as well as the complexity of functions and data required clear rules for all attributes of screen display and interaction. Our firm provided this guidance. In the limited scope of this section it is not possible to provide details on the many aspects of screen display, window detailing, typography, color, cursors, and interaction. I shall concentrate on a key feature, the icons themselves (see Fig. 3.8 for a revised

Figure 3.9 Examples of
Icon Lexicon Elements

The figures show how
standard elements of icons
are to be drawn.

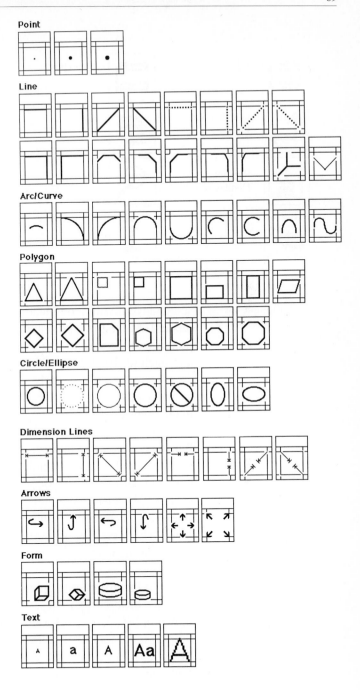

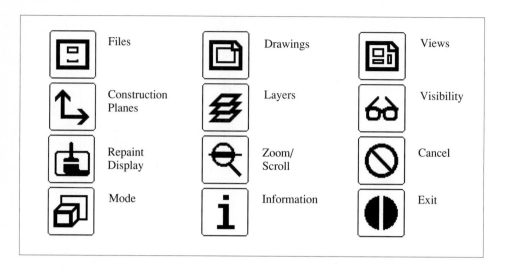

Figure 3.10 Examples of Revised Global-Command Icons

screen layout with icon location indicated within the menus). At the time, with approximately a dozen modules in the system, the number of icons was approaching 10,000 and Computervision staff were creating more daily. Clearly, everyone involved needed to understand the basic rules for icon design and layout in the menus.

Because of the large number of icons and the complexity of the symbolic or illustrative contents within the icon, the outline and intericon spacing were treated very simply: there are no three-dimensional or shaded sides, there is merely a single outline with a place for a seven-letter verbal equivalent to the visual symbol at the top of the icon.

To assist the group of people designing individual icons for different modules, we created the icon lexicon shown in Fig. 3.9. This lexicon provided a practical, simple, consistent kit of parts with which to construct any icon. By using the kit of icon parts, the design staff could maintain appearance standards with greater ease.

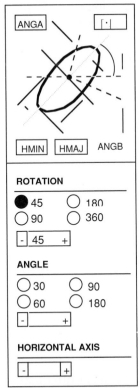

Figure 3.11 Additional
Examples of Revised Icons

To provide guidance for composite symbols, we also designed a starter set of icons that could be used for the global commands. This set appears in Fig. 3.10. The general features of these symbols (see also Fig. 3.11) helped to show the Computervision staff the correct approach to treatment of detail, curves, angles, visual density, and depiction of objects.

The examples in Fig. 3.11 show symbolism for "supericons" and icon classification according to treatment of subicons or subcommands.

We proposed a special addition to the visual syntax of icon appearance in order to help operators understand the semantics of different kinds of icons. Depending on the class of icon, selecting an individual icon can lead to different display/action sequences:

Direct activation of an icon
Appearance of a submenu page
Appearance of a pulldown menu
Appearance of an additional window
Toggle of an icon state

In the previous design, small symbols appeared within the nonverbal part of the icon to indicate these different semantics. We suggested treating the top edge of the verbal part of the icon with a characteristic pattern that would signify uniquely this kind of icon. This approach did not decrease the legibility of the alphanumerics and helped keep the nonverbal part of the icon less cluttered.

These changes in menu appearance are only one aspect of the recommendations for appearance and interaction within the user interface. These recommendations indicate the amount of attention to details that good user-interface design requires. These small improvements added together increase the effectiveness and communicative quality of the user interface.

Conclusion

The achievements of the Computervision user-interface manual in the design process of the CADD Station owe much to the insight and support of the then Computervision staff, especially Kevin Sullivan, Carl Jacobsen, and Scott Sipherd, who provided initial guidance and review, and to Michael Arent and Bruce Browne formerly of our firm who created the final detailed specifications. The manual helped Computervision to achieve quality visual communication and a cost-effective consistency of design. Computervision's own internal evaluation of the success of this approach is an indication that the approach can benefit other manufacturers and other application areas.

3.4 An Annotated Bibliography of Signs, Icons, and Symbols

Introduction

The design of signs, icons, and symbols is currently one of the weaker visual aspects of electronic publishing and user interfaces. User interfaces, information graphics, and electronic publishing systems offer users the opportunity to display objects, processes, and data as nonverbal signs. The most complex graphics workstations require users to learn hundreds or even thousands of different symbols.

Professional graphic designers have traditionally dealt with these features but today the division of labor is less clear. The responsibility for design frequently falls upon the developer or user of a computer graphics system. Software automates part of the process but cannot select the right kind of sign and design it properly.

In a few cases, there are libraries of signs for a limited variety of meanings and graphic editing tools. Experience, imagination, and skill are still the designer's most essential assets, for these will determine the quality of the final design. Fortunately, there are a number of helpful references, like those listed below. These sources provide excellent advice on issues, principles, recommendations, and case studies for what to do when designing icons and symbols of all kinds. Unfortunately some of the best books are the hardest to obtain, because they are not usually located in one part of a library or one kind of bookstore. It may take some effort to find them, but they can be a valuable resource.

Recommended Publications

Aicher, Otto, and Martin Krampen, *Zeichensysteme der Visuellen Kommunikation* (Sign Systems of Visual Communication), Alexander Koch Publishers, Stuttgart, 1977, ISBN 3-87422-565-8, 154 pp. The authors, who are an outstanding graphic designer and graphic design analyst, provide a handbook for designers, architects, and planners. The book provides detailed visual examples and explanation.

American Institute of Graphic Arts, *Symbol Signs*, Visual Communication Books, Hastings House, New York 1981, ISBN 0-8038-6777-8, 240 pp. For the U.S. Department of Transportation, a team of graphic designers analyzed and evaluated 28 sources of mass transportation signs.

Arnstein, J., *The International Dictionary of Graphic Symbols,* Kogan Page Ltd., Whitstable, Kent, England, 1983, ISBN 0-85038-578-4, 239 pp. This is a handbook for identifying and understanding graphic symbols. Black-and-white examples in 30 categories, from electronics and engineering to heraldry and politics, appear with their denotations and, in some cases, brief additional explanations.

Bliss, C.K., *Semantography,* Semantography (Blissymbolics) Publications, Sydney, Australia, 1965, 882 pp. In this classic work by a well-known pioneer in the field, the author presents his system of graphic signs for universal communication.

Cirlot, J.E., *A Dictionary of Symbols,* trans. J. Sage, Philosophical Library, New York, 1962, 400 pp. The author presents a scholarly discussion of Eastern and Western symbols used in art and literature, which are organized in alphabetical order.

Diethelm, Walter, with M. Diethelm, *Signet, Signal, Symbol,* ABC Verlag, Zurich, 1970, 226 pp. The authors present a graphic designer's view of well-designed signs in approximately 10 subject categories. They also include a glossary and semiotic classification.

Dreyfuss, Henry, *Symbol Sourcebook,* McGraw-Hill, New York, 1972, ISBN 07-017837-2, 292 pp. The author, a designer of international reputation, presents a catalogue of examples in 26 subject categories. In addition, this highly recommended book presents a section organized by graphic form, some symbolic denotations, connotations of color, and a detailed bibliography of sources.

Green, Paul, and W.T. Burgess, "Debugging a Symbol Set for Identifying Displays: Production and Screening Studies," Tech. report UM-HSRI-80-64, Highway Safety Research Institute, September 1980, 116 pp., available through NTIS, no. PB81-113573. This report shows how to conduct human factors testing of signs.

Jung, Carl G., *Man and his Symbols,* Doubleday and Co., Garden City, NY, 1964, ISBN 0-385-05221-9, 320 pp. This respected psychologist is noted for his theory of archetypal symbols.

Kuyayama, Y., *Trademarks & Symbols,* 2 vols., Van Nostrand Reinhold Co., New York, 1973. Vol. 1: ISBN 0-442-24563-7, 193 pp.; Vol. 2: ISBN 0-442-24563-7, 186 pp. This two-volume set, typical of trademark catalogues, presents approximately 3000 black-and-white examples of registered commercial signs.

Lerner, N.D., and B.L. Collins, "The Assessment of Safety Symbol Understandability by Different Testing Methods," U.S. Department of Commerce, Natural Bureau of Standards, Environmental Design Research Division, August 1980, 51 pp. The report shows useful test results and describes methodology.

Modley, Rudolf, with William R. Myers, *Handbook of Pictorial Symbols,* Dover Publications, New York, 1976, ISBN 0-486-23357-X, 143 pp. The author presents black-and-white examples of approximately 3000 graphic signs.

Neurath, O., *International Picture Language,* University of Reading, England, 1980, 70 pp. This publication is a facsimile reprint of the 1936 English edition of Neurath's explanation of the isotype system of pictographic signs.

Ota, Y., "LoCoS: An Experimental Pictorial Language," *Icographic*, no. 6, 1973, pp. 15-19. This is a quarterly review of international visual-communication design, published by the International Council of Graphic Design Associations (ICOGRADA), POB 398, London W11-4UG, England. This is one of the few explanations in English of the author's system of universal visual-sign communication.

Shepherd, W., *Shepherd's Glossary of Graphic Signs and Symbols,* Dover Publications, New York, 1971, ISBN 0-486-20700-5, 587 pp. This reference lists thousands of symbols by professional categories.

"Signs and Display Systems, Graphic Design, and Human Engineering," PB82-808585, U.S. Department of Commerce, National Technical Information Service, June 1982, 170 pp. This reference provides useful human factors guidance.

Smeets, R., *Signs, Symbols & Ornaments,*
Van Nostrand Reinhold Co., New York, 1982, ISBN
0-442-27800-4, 176 pp. This reference provides numerous fanciful and historical examples of signs.

Weilgart, J.W., *AUI: The Language of Space,* 1974,
341 pp. and *Cosmic Elements of Meaning: Symbols of the Spirit's Life,* 1975, 303 pp. Published by Cosmic
Communication Co., Decorah, IA. The author presents
his own system of 31 symbols and sounds for universal
communication.

Chapter 4 Color

Color is the most sophisticated and complex of the visible language components. We react strongly to color in the natural environment, in graphic communication, in architecture, and in industrial design. As color hardcopy devices and color display screens proliferate, a skilled, professional use of color must accompany all communication.

4.1 The Ten Commandments of Color

Introduction

Within the computer graphics industry, one of the most significant changes in the past decade has been the increased use of color displays on CRT screens, on overhead foils, in film and slides, and on paper. Terminals, personal computers, and workstations are ablaze with color, and color hardcopy devices of all kinds are becoming more common.

What Is Color?

Color scientists, artists, and designers describe color phenomena in different terms. One useful set of terms is hue, value, and chroma (Fig. 4.1).

Hue: The spectral wavelength composition of a color that produces perceptions of being blue, orange, brown, etc.

Value: The relative amount of lightness or darkness of the color in a range of black to white (also called intensity).

Figure 4.1
Color Relationships

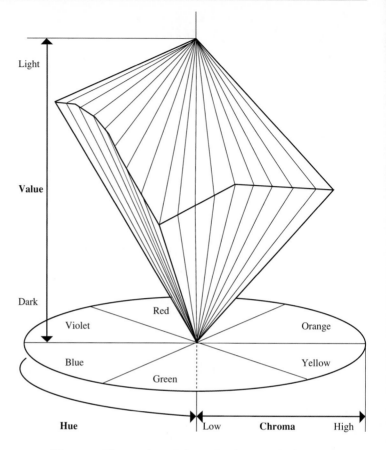

Chroma: The purity of the color in a scale from gray to the most vivid variant of the perceived color (also called saturation).

As shown in Fig. 4.1, primary colors of illuminated light such as red, blue, and green combine additively (that is, all wavelengths being included) in pairs to produce magenta, cyan, and yellow. Mixed together, these colors make white light. Primary colors of pigment color such as red, blue, and yellow (or magenta, cyan, and yellow) combine together subtractively (that is, excluding all wavelengths) to make a dark brown-black. Typical four-color printing processes of images on paper uses optical mixtures, which are closely spaced small dots of primary colors of magenta, cyan, and yellow plus black, to achieve " full-color " printing. CRT

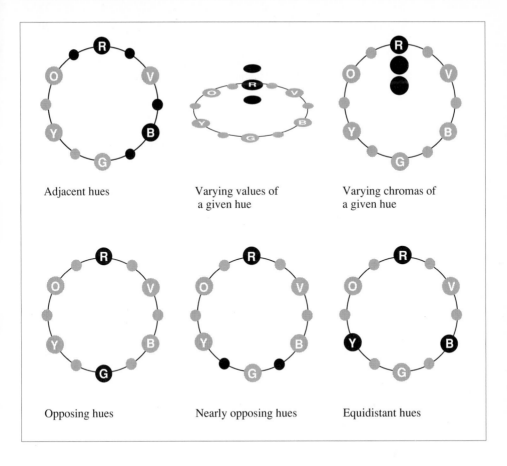

| Adjacent hues | Varying values of a given hue | Varying chromas of a given hue |

| Opposing hues | Nearly opposing hues | Equidistant hues |

Figure 4.2 Color Mixtures

screens typically combine light additively, while most other color is obtained through subtractive mixtures of pigments, dyes, or tints.

The diagrams in Fig. 4.2 depict typical means of achieving clearly related sets of colors. Adjacent hues are sections of the hue circle, such as the so-called warm colors (red-orange, red, red-violet) or cool colors (blue-violet, blue, blue-green). Varying values of a given hue are the so-called monochromatic colors (dark red, medium-value red, light red).Varying chromas of a given hue include dull red, medium-chroma red, and pure red. Opposing hues are the so-called complementary colors opposite each other on the hue circle (red, green). Nearly opposing hues are the so-called split-complementary colors comprising a hue and the two hues adjacent to its complement (red, blue-green, yellow-green). Equidistant hues are the so-called triadic colors equally spaced around the hue circle (red, blue, yellow).

What Can Color Do?   Let us first acknowledge what color can accomplish. Color can offer the following advantages:

- Call attention to specific data or information

- Identify elements of structures and processes

- Portray natural objects realistically

- Depict the logical structure of ideas and processes

- Portray time and progress

- Increase appeal, believability, memorability, and comprehensibility

- Reduce errors of legibility or interpretation

- Increase the number of dimensions for coding data

- Show qualities and quantities in a limited space

  At the same time, color has these potential drawbacks or disadvantages:

- Requires more expensive and complicated display equipment

- May not account for color deficient vision among some viewers (about 8 percent of Caucasian males)

- May cause visual fatigue and after images induced by strong colors

- May contribute to visual confusion due to complexity and potency of color phenomena

• May have negative cultural or historical associations

• May exhibit confusing cross-disciplinary and cross-cultural connotations

Need for Guidelines   Despite the increased availability of color in the industry, the understanding and effective use of color has progressed more modestly. Developers and users of color computer graphics displays often ask the following questions:

Which colors should I use?
How many colors should I use?
Are these colors appropriate?
How can I improve them?

There is a need for recommendations on the use of color for computer graphics displays. Establishing general rules or specifications for color use is difficult: we lack some important understanding about the nature of color vision, and the factors that influence specific color choices are diverse. Nevertheless, concise, useful recommendations can be formulated. Some general guidelines have appeared in the computer graphics industry's trade and professional magazines (see Section 4.2 and the Bibliography, Section 4.1).

Basis for the Ten   For this section, I have examined a number of these
Commandments   articles and have synthesized the information contained in them. Summarizing the articles has not always been a simple task; the published guidelines themselves seem occasionally to offer opposite recommendations. For example, with respect to opponent color combinations (those colors that represent the system used to code color differences in the optic nerve: yellow-blue, red-green, and white-black), an article by Murch (Bibliography, Section 4.1) states, "Opponent colors go well together," while Durett and Trezona (Bibliography, Section 4.1) state, "...opponent-color

combinations should always be avoided." Usually there is a way to resolve the differences, and the articles generally corroborate each other's assertions. I have also added some insights gained from our firm's own experience in planning, designing, and producing color user interfaces and information displays in a variety of media.

The reader must be cautioned that the advice offered here is not always supported by references to precise, accurate scientific evaluation. Furthermore, the emphasis is on explicit coding of information and optimum discrimination rather than on conveying realism, mood, or other aesthetic qualities. I have tried to make the recommendations suitable for most media. These guidelines are not listed in order of importance. These "Ten Commandments" are grouped together with supplementary exhortations into an arrangement based loosely on semiotics. The sequence emphasizes syntactics (rules for number, size, arrangement, and contrast), semantics (rules for referencing, or denotation and connotation), and pragmatics (rules for intentions, responses, and preferences). Discussion is provided on each rule based on physiological, perceptual, and cognitive issues.

1. Use a maximum of five plus or minus two colors.

To the general question "How many?", the general answer is invariably seven plus or minus two (as explained in Section 2.2). But with respect to color, it seems best to be conservative. For novice viewers, four distinct colors are appropriate. This amount allows extra room in short-term memory (about 20 seconds), which can store five words or shapes, six letters, seven colors, and eight digits. For aesthetic purposes such as design style, emotional expression, or realism, more colors will be required. Although some computer CRT display equipment can provide 16 million or more colors and the average human being can discriminate about 7.5 million colors, this simple rule radically reduces the complexity of the problem for that medium.

Use spectral order in color coding. To order a large set of colors, use the the spectral sequence ROY G BIV (red, orange, yellow, green, blue, indigo, violet). Tests have shown that viewers see a spectral order as a natural one and would select red, green, and blue (cyan) as intuitive choices for the front, middle, and back layers respectively, when viewing a multilayer circuit board (see Bibliography, Section 4.1, Fromme 1983).

2. Use foveal (central) and peripheral colors appropriately.

Use blue for large areas, not for text type, thin lines, or small shapes. In the eye's retina, blue-sensitive cones are the least numerous of the color receptors, and the fovea, the eye's central focusing area, contains relatively few of these blue-sensitive cones. Blue is good for slide and screen backgrounds.

Use red and green in the center of the visual field, not in the periphery. The edges of the retina are not particularly sensitive to these colors. If they are used at the periphery, some signal to the viewer must be given to capture attention, for example, size change, blinking, etc.

Use black, white, yellow, and blue in the periphery of the visual field. The retina remains sensitive to these colors in the periphery.

Use adjacent colors that differ by hue and value. Do not use adjacent colors that differ only in the amount of blue. The dearth of blue cones is again responsible for this rule. The edge between the two colors will seem fuzzy.

3. Use a color area that exhibits a minimum shift in color and/or size if the color area changes in size.

As they decrease in size, color areas appear to change their value and chroma. Consequently, color interactions with the background fields become more pronounced. In addition, illusions of similar colors from different colors, or vice-versa can appear.

Use light text, thin lines, and small shapes (white, yellow, or red) on medium-dark and dark backgrounds (blue, green, red, or dark gray) for dark viewing situations. Long distance or low ambient-light viewing situations are used typically for slide presentations, workstations, video, etc. Video displays require colors that are lower chroma (less saturation). Reserve the highest contrast in figure-field relationships for text type.

Use dark text, thin lines, and small shapes (blue or black) on light backgrounds (light yellow, magenta, green, blue, or white) for light viewing situations. Typical viewing situations are those for overhead transparencies, paper, etc. Reserve the highest contrast in figure field relationships for text type.

4. Do not use simultaneously high-chroma, spectrally extreme colors.

For figure-figure and many figure-field relationships, strong contrasts of red/green, blue/yellow, green/blue, and red/blue create vibrations, illusions of shadows, and after-images.

5. Use familiar, consistent color codings with appropriate references.

Common Western denotations are the following:

Red: stop, danger, hot, fire
Yellow: caution, slow, test
Green: go, okay, clear, vegetation, safety
Blue: cold, water, calm, sky
Warm colors: action, response required, proximity
Cool colors: status, background information, distance
Grays, white, and blue: neutrality

Use color for quantitative coding as well as for qualitative coding. For example, in chart or diagram displays, the degree of color change can be linked to some magnitude change in the displayed process or event. This redundant coding can help clarify and emphasize the meaning of the chart or diagram. Color change can also replace bar or line charts, for example, when the viewer is interested in current status or trends, not in history. A single small area changing in color rather than a bar or line can save space.

Use color connotations with great care. Connotations vary greatly among different viewers. For example, consider some of the American connotations of the color blue:

For movie audiences: tenderness, pornography
For financial managers: corporate qualities, reliability
For health-care professionals: death
For nuclear-reactor monitors: coolness, water

Some typical associations of color with dramatic portrayal include the following:

High illumination: hot, active, comic

Low illumination: emotional, tense, tragic, melodramatic, romantic

High chroma: emotional, tense, hot, comic, melodramatic

Warm hues: (red, orange, and yellow) activity, comedy, leisure, recreation

Cool hues: (green, blue, violet, purple, and gray) tragedy, romance, efficiency, work

The correct use of color requires careful analysis of the experience and expectations of the viewers.

6. Use the same color for grouping related elements.

Do not use a particular color for any element that is *not* related to the other elements. A viewer can sense relations by color over space and over time (in sequences of images); consequently, it is important to be complete and consistent in color grouping. Command and control colors in menus, for example, should not be used for information coding within a work area, unless a specific connection is intended. Similar background colors of related areas can subtly orient the viewer to recognize the conceptual linking of the two areas without other more explicit cues.

7. Use the same color code for training, testing, application, and publication.

Once color coding is established, the same colors should be used throughout the life cycle of knowledge generation and dissemination. This color continuity may require the colors to appear in different media. This transference will necessitate careful selection of colors that can be displayed consistently across media with differing techniques for generating color. Note that CRT screens use additive color mixtures, which combine into white, while most hardcopy devices use subtractive color mixtures, which combine into black. The color gamuts (available color ranges) of these two media are not identical.

8. Use high-value, high-chroma colors to attract attention.

The use of bright colors for danger signals, attention getters, reminders, cursors, etc. is entirely appropriate. High-chroma red alerts seem to aid faster response than yellow or yellow-orange. When too many figures or background fields compete for the viewer's attention, confusion arises. The hierarchy of highlighted, neutral, and lowlighted states for all areas of the visual display must be carefully designed to maximize simplicity and clarity.

Use brighter color for older viewers or for those who have viewed displays for long periods of time. Older viewers need higher brightness levels to help distinguish colors. Over long viewing periods, even younger viewers lose the ability to distinguish colors, and some increase in brightness may be required for extended periods of viewing.

9. Use redundant coding of shape, as well as color, if possible.

This approach aids viewers with color-deficient vision and makes the display more resilient to color distortions caused by ambient-light changes or by medium-to- medium conversion. Ambient-light changes can cause changes in perceived hue, value, and chroma.

10. Use color to enhance black-and-white information.

With respect to learning and comprehension, color is superior to black-and-white in terms of the viewer's processing time and emotional reactions, but there is no difference in a viewer's ability to interpret information. In other words, people do not learn more from a color display, but they may think they do. The crucial factor, however, is that color is more enjoyable. Memory for color information also appears to be superior to that for black-and-white.

Using These Recommendations

While these "Ten Commandments" may not solve most of the precise color selection problems that manufacturers and users face, they may be able to point people in the right direction. It is worth the effort to make available this information at all computer graphics installations.

It is more helpful to put the commandments into action and to publish useful color palettes or color templates that users, including the color deficient, may adopt (or adapt) in selecting and applying colors. Most users do not know how to select color for type and symbols; how to draw the eye's attention to particular elements without creating a chaotic or unfocused composition; or how to apply color to different applications and media, such as tables, forms, pages, and screens effectively. While some users may have special skills in color selection or use, many users feel they have neither the talent nor the time to select colors. For large organizations, it maximizes efficiency to provide users with preselected color standards that meet general and specific user needs.

These preselected color standards can provide detailed color solutions to designing graphic elements such as cursors, title bars, window backgrounds, and icon colors of user interfaces, as well as the typical elements of printed documents including titles, captions, marginalia. More sophisticated highlighting symbols, such as ruled lines in titles and tables also benefit. Even compositions of prototype charts, diagrams, or screen layouts could be enhanced. Within any organization, supplying this assistance in printed documentation or online help can improve the quality of design and increase productivity. This functional approach can also establish a corporate identity and corporate-wide standards of quality communication.

In-house graphic design groups or outside consultants can develop color standards and specifications for applications and can make the information available to those who seek this assistance. If the organization has a corporate graphics group, the creation of color standards and guidelines for the application and composition of color can be accomplished in-house. In some cases, the corporate defaults, conventions, or standards may simply emerge from one enterprising department's production staff.

One of the keys to real productivity is achieving the power of communication effectiveness (as well as time savings in production) made possible with pre-established graphics. If these graphics are designed well, everyone benefits: the senders, the receivers, and the equipment that makes it all possible. Once again, this approach is a significant opportunity for the graphic design profession to work closely with the computer graphics community to achieve truly high-quality visual communication.

In the not too distant future, I believe we shall see some of this color information embodied in computer-based expert systems that contain much of the detailed knowledge of color science and graphic design. These systems will have the ability to apply that knowledge to the problem at hand. A color expert could help resolve such problems as the differences in the color needs for an executive and a sales staff member. A complete system will have to account for each of the varying color requirements of research, development, operations, production, marketing, and distribution, as well as for the eventual user of computer graphics-based knowledge generation and dissemination. Developing color design assistance will make it possible for us all to benefit from the world's expert designers and to communicate through color more efficiently and effectively.

Color Issues

Beyond the existing or potential value of color in information graphics and user interfaces, many questions need to be answered. Here are some of the issues that surround the use of color. Some of them have been researched while many remain unresolved.

Which colors aid safety and error-free recognition?

Which colors aid precise visual performance?

Which colors contribute to physical or psychological fatigue?

Which colors reduce monotony? boredom? stress?

Which colors enhance the perception of leisure time, and which reduce the perception of work time?

Which colors contribute to a natural appearance of people, objects, or environments?

Which colors have the strongest/weakest impact on cultural reactions?

Which colors are typically used to denote certain functions, activities, or objects?

Which colors affect impressions of temperature and humidity?

Which colors are acceptable to the largest group of people in the intended audience?

Which colors aid orientation?

Which colors help balance human needs with human desires?

Which colors will a multicultural group find clearly distinct? appropriate? attractive?

Which colors produce short-term and long-term changes in the human body?

Which colors promote involvement in group activities?

Which colors control conformity versus independence?

Which colors do men or women prefer? Should any differences be reflected in coloring of products and services rendered through computer graphics displays?

Which colors can be used to create apparent movement?

Which colors optimize productivity?

Should users/viewers be able to change generic or standard colors? How?

How can color be used to symbolize or ritualize time? play graphics? work graphics?

Which colors affect human biological daily or annual rhythms?

Do traditional references of colors need to be maintained? What have other cultures and other historical periods used?

How should color interact with typography, texture, and sound?

Conclusion　　　　Color hardcopy devices and display screens are increasing their use of color. As color depiction becomes stable and legibility factors become settled, more subtle and complex issues will become important. For example, in office automation, is it possible to establish generic color associations for the essential informational, social, and psychological dimensions of productive office activities? Specialists, such as human-factors engineers and graphic designers, will have increasing amounts of experience to share with programmers, managers, marketers, and users who will need answers to these intriguing questions. For the present, individual programmers and users will have to seek out some answers themselves or turn to the limited number of specialists looking into these issues.

4.2 An Annotated Bibliography of Color

Introduction　　　　The availability of relatively inexpensive color workstations, decreasing prices, and increasing quality of color hardcopy devices makes this an exciting time for people in the computer graphics industry. Developing ways to communicate facts, concepts, and emotions to persuade, inform, and aesthetically please the viewer is a major challenge for contemporary workstation design. This publication list provides a starting point for analysis, planning, design, and production of color displays. Sources for many of these references are identified in Section 1.3.

Equipped with the background that these books provide, programmers, managers, writers, and all those suddenly involved with developing and using information graphics on CRTs, on slide screens, and in publications can make better decisions about complex color graphics. The result will be higher visual quality in terms of communication effectiveness.

As more computer graphics systems move toward color display, the industry will gradually produce more high-quality, appropriate literature for developers and users. In the past few years, a number of new publications have appeared that provide practical advice. This trend can be expected to continue.

Recommended Publications

Albers, Josef, *Interaction of Color,* Yale University Press, New Haven, 1975, 81 pp. The author, a noted artist and teacher, presents his analysis of color interaction and composition phenomena in a classic, illustrated text for art and design students.

Barker, E., and M. J. Krebs, *Color Coding Effects on Human Performance, An Annotated Bibliography,* U.S. Office of Naval Research, Arlington, VA, April 1977, 91 pp. The authors examines 78 studies and articles on the effects of color as a coding dimension in various tasks.

Berlin, B., and P. Kay, *Basic Color Terms,* University of California Press, Berkeley, 1969, 178 pp. The authors, both anthropologists, explain their study of 98 languages and their discovery of 11 basic color terms that have a distinct sequence of emergence in human languages.

Birren, Faber, *Color and Human Response,* Van Nostrand Reinhold Co., New York, 1978, 0-442-20787-5, 141 pp., few illustrations. One of the leading authorities discusses not only biological and visual response to color, but emotional, aesthetic and psychic reactions.

——*Principles of Color,* Van Nostrand Reinhold Co., New York, 1969, ISBN 0-442-20774-3, 96 pp., eight color illustrations. This leading authority reviews past traditions and modern theories of color harmony.

Chevreul, M.E., *The Principles of Harmony and Contrast of Colors and Their Applications to the Arts,* Van Nostrand Reinhold Co, New York, 1981, ISBN 0-442-2121207, 224 pp., large format. This translation of Chevreul's classic edition of 1839 introduces the theories that influenced the Impressionist and Neo-Impressionist painters. His scientific principles became part of basic color training in art and design schools.

Chijiwa, H., *Color Harmony,* Rockport Publishers, Rockport, MA, 1987, ISBN 0-935603-06-9, 158 pp. The author presents a series of basic colors and a series of combination schemes based on such terms as "striking," "natural," "feminine," and "surprising." Many practical applications are also shown.

"Consumer Color Charts, Munsell Color," Kollmorgen Corp., Macbeth Division, Baltimore, 16 pp., plus charts. This brochure explains the Munsell color system.

Cowan, William B., *Color Research and Application*, special ed., Vol. 11, 1986, 92 pp. This special edition of an important publication for historical scientific and cultural information about color represents the proceedings of an Association Internationale de la Coleur Interim Meeting on Color in Computer Generated Displays held in Toronto, June 1986.

de Grandis, Luigina, *Theory and Use of Color,* trans. A. Mondadori, Harry N. Abrams, New York, 1984, ISBN 0-8109-2317-3, 159 pp. The author presents his explanation of physiological and perceptual phenomena with large color illustrations. He also presents some composition principles.

Itten, Josef, *The Art of Color,* Van Nostrand Reinhold Co., New York, 1973, ISBN 0-422-24037-6, 155 pp., large format. This internationally known artist and teacher presents his theory of color organization, contrasts, harmony and expression in a profusely illustrated book.

——*The Elements of Color,* Van Nostrand Reinhold Co., New York, 1970, ISBN 0-442-24038-4, 95 pp. This treatise is an edited version of the author's more complete book, *The Art of Color*. This volume explains Itten's theory of color elements, contrast, composition, and harmony.

Kelly, K.L., and D.B. Judd, *Color: Universal Language and Dictionary of Names,* U.S. Department of Commerce, National Bureau of Standards, December 1976, 158 pp. no. 003-003-01705-1. The authors present their revisions of the Universal Color Language for designating colors verbally and a Munsell-correlated dictionary of 7000 commercial color names.

Kobayashi, S., with R. Sternberg, *A Book of Colors,* Kodansha International, Harper Row, New York, 1987, ISBN 0-87011-800-5, 128 pp. This small paperback (by the founder and director of the Nippon Color and Design Research Institute) presents preselected palettes of colors organized by subject and color themes.

Kuehni, R.G., *Color: Essence and Logic,* Van Nostrand Reinhold Co., New York, 1983, 138 pp. The author, a color technical expert, seeks to provide a nontechnical account of all aspects of color, including colorimetry and reproduction. He includes an appendix tracing the historical evolution of color ideas.

Kueppers, H., *Color Atlas,* Barron's Educational Series, Inc. Woodbury, NY, 1982, ISBN 0-8120-2172-X, 170 pp. This handbook shows the mixing possibilities of three- and four-color printing in uniform gradations. These color charts can be used as a reliable reference source. The book is *not* a work on color theory.

——*Color: Origin, Systems, Users,* trans. F. Bradley, Van Nostrand Reinhold Co., New York, 1972, ISBN 0-442-29985-0, 155 pp, 86 illustrations. The author presents a systematic description and explanation of psychological and perceptual color theory.

Lamberski, Richard J., "A Comprehensive and Critical Review of the Methodology and Findings in Color Investigations," *Proc. Annual Convention of the Association of Educational Communications and Technology*, no. ED-194063/IR008916, Association for Educational Communications & Technology, Denver, CO, April 1980, pp. 338-379. The author reviews existing literature relating to cognitive processing and color as a cue or code strategy. His findings are controversial: due to limited experimental evidence, color's role in cognitive functioning is not clear.

Marx, E., *Optical Color and Simultaneity,* trans. Geoffrey O'Brien, Van Nostrand Reinhold Co., New York, 1983, ISBN 0-442-23864-9, 152 pp. The author explains a system of color combinations based on optical mixtures (reflective surfaces with small elements of color as in color halftone printing) and provides a viewing apparatus to demonstrate her principles.

Munsell, A.H., *A Grammar of Color, ed.* F. Birren, Van Nostrand Reinhold Co., New York, 1969, LC 69-15896, 96 pp. The author presents his theory of color organization, identification, and harmony. This system is well-known to artists, designers, and manufacturers.

Ostwald, William, *The Color Primer,* ed. F. Birren, Van Nostrand Reinhold Co., New York, 1969, LC 69-15897, 96 pp., eight color illustrations. In this important historical document, Ostwald presents his theory of color relations.

"Pantone Color Guide," Pantone, Inc., Moonachie, NJ. This document and other color reference manuals explain and demonstrated the Pantone Matching System (PMS). This set, like that of Munsell, is well-established among artists, designers, and manufacturers of colors.

"Process Color Guide," 2d ed., S.D. Scott Printing Co., New York, 1986, 96 pp., large format. A high-quality printing company presents almost 5000 two-and three-color process ink tint combinations on coated and flat white paper to demonstrate the wide range of colors that can be produced and to provide a basis for color matching.

Rossotti, H., *Colour,* Princeton University Press, Princeton, 1983, ISBN 0-691-02386-7, 239 pp. The author, a chemist, presents a complete discussion of color phenomena, mechanisms, and principles.

Rowell, J., *Picture Perfect: Color Output for Computer Graphics,* Tecktronix Inc., Beaverton, OR, 1990, Part No. 070-6559-00. This basic introduction contains many full-color computer graphics examples.

Sloane, P., *Color: Basic Principles and New Directions,* Reinhold Studio Vista, London, 1968. This reference provides a basic introduction to theory for artists and designers.

Southworth, M., *Pocket Guide to Color Reproduction: Communication and Control*, Graphic Arts Publishing Co., Livonia, NY, 1979, ISBN 0-933600-01-1, 106 pp. This pocket book, by a faculty member of the School of Printing of Rochester Institute of Technology, explains color reproduction processes, standard viewing conditions, and evaluation issues for transparencies, color proofs, and printing. This practical guide also includes references and a glossary.

Thorell, Lisa G., and Wanda J. Smith, *Using Computer Color Effectively,* Prentice Hall, Inc., Englewood Cliffs, NJ, 1990. This thorough reference work provides many color examples and detailed human-factors data.

Chapter 5   Visualizing Knowledge: Charts, Diagrams, and Maps

Communicating structure and process effectively is the unique capability of charts, maps, and diagrams. In electronic documents and user interfaces laden with data, appropriate visualizations can provide different perspectives, details, summaries and overviews, generalizations, and trends. These visible language devices filter knowledge and provide appropriate "chunking," hierarchy, and pacing. Charts, diagrams, and maps are increasingly relied upon to help manage large quantities of information. Design expertise can make these knowledge visualizations even more effective.

5.1 Chart Design

Introduction

Chart-making business graphics systems use increasingly sophisticated typography, and high-resolution, multicolor hardcopy and screen displays. Builders and users of these systems need to recognize some of the basic issues of legibility and readability in designing and applying these graphic forms. Legibility concerns the reader's ability to successfully find, identify, and absorb what the chart denotes. Readability concerns the chart's interpretation and appeal. Studies have shown that both legibility and readability can be significantly improved through careful selection of graphic elements and layout of the material.

Business graphics have benefited from many of the graphic design advances in computer graphics technology: varieties of charts, high-resolution display, multifont typography, and full-spectrum color. In the past few years, the cost of equipment to generate and record quality business graphics has declined. At the same time, integrated software packages are enabling spreadsheet users to look at data in chart form. As chart making becomes a routine function of executive information systems (EIS), decision support systems (DSS), and data management/display, good communication with charts must also become a routine skill of computer users in the business graphics community.

More than ever, there is a need to be clear about the advantages and graphic design issues of good chart making. How can we best use business charts? What should they look like? This section answers these questions.

Why Use Charts?   One of the major problems of the information age is that we are drowning in all the information we receive. Luckily, the computer can help solve the problem it creates. Masses of data otherwise presented as lengthy prose or in tabular form can be converted into charts, sometimes at the press of a button and in a blink of an eye.

It was only a few hundred years ago that William Playfair and other pioneers introduced chart making as we know it today. Computer graphics systems have added sophisticated visual capabilities, but the basic value of charts remains the same: they can present patterns or trends in data clearly, quickly, and efficiently, especially with respect to change over time. Charts facilitate identification and comparison of data values that would be cumbersome or impossible in other data formats. Their visual form makes it easy to highlight data and to make data readable or inviting.

Before examining the kinds of charts and how to design them, it is appropriate to recognize the fundamental differences in the communication goals for charts. There are two reasons for using charts in business graphics: to understand a situation and to convey that understanding to the audience. We can distinguish these two modes as problem solving versus presentation.

The audience can be the persons creating the chart or their fellow team members, or another group, such as management, support staff, a research team, or the general public. These kinds of audiences are distinguished as personal, peer, and public.

Mode and audience affect what we say and how we say it visually, just as we alter our speech or writing for different audiences. Generally, we accept more informal methods of display for problem solving and for personal- and peer-review graphics. We are more demanding about style and finely tuned displays for presentation graphics, especially to the general public. Of course, there is always a need to be accurate, simple, clear, and concise when we choose the right chart for the right data.

Although statisticians, scientists, and engineers have invented many fascinating forms of charts, the business community currently prefers a limited set of charts: line charts, bar charts, and pie charts. Let us look at each of these kinds of charts.

Line Charts

Line charts, also called curve charts, like the one pictured in Fig. 5.1 connect data points on a measurable area (usually a Cartesian grid) to show one dependent data variable plotted against an independent variable (often time). In this method it is easy to show long series of data, to interpolate between points, to extrapolate beyond the known data values, and to compare several data lines. The purpose of using a line chart is to emphasize a trend, rather than actual amounts. Usually these charts are arithmetic, that is, each axis scale is measured in equal, easily countable segments.

Figure 5.1 Line Chart

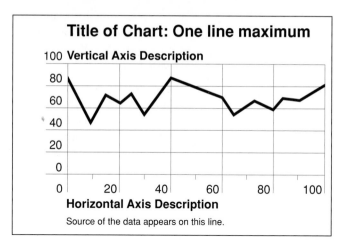

Figure 5.2 Semilogarithmic
Line Chart

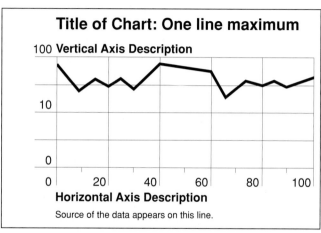

There is another kind of line chart called the semilogarithmic chart as pictured in Fig. 5.2, whose dependent
axis is measured in the unusual repeating pattern of the
logarithm of data values. This line chart is extremely
useful when we are looking for relative changes in data
values that vary greatly. The arithmetic line chart is
more useful when the data values are approximately the
same order of magnitude. Although some important
phenomena can be shown clearly with semilogarithmic
line charts, many people are not familiar with their format. They should be used with great care, and explanatory information should accompany them. Another
important variation on the typical line chart is the 100

Figure 5.3 100 Percent
Line Chart

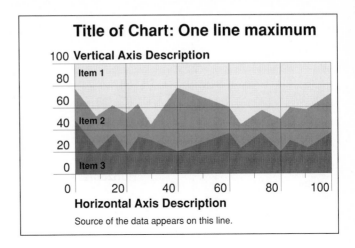

Title of Chart: One line maximum

100 **Vertical Axis Description**

80 Item 1

60

40 Item 2

20

0   Item 3

    0   20   40   60   80   100

Horizontal Axis Description

Source of the data appears on this line.

percent surface chart as shown in Fig. 5.3, which allows us to emphasize components of a whole.

In designing line charts, make the data lines the thick-
est lines in the chart and the grid lines thin or even ab-
sent. The axes should be of a medium weight and
should be part of a rectangle that defines the entire data
area. If there is sufficient space around the data area,
the tick marks and scale values should be placed outside this area. If several data lines appear, these must
be distinguished clearly by texture and/or color. Avoid
presenting more than five data lines. Care should be
taken that the lines overlap with a clear spatial order,
without accidentally mixing textures or colors. For
maximum legibility, keep all typography horizontal if
possible. Sans serif type in a single font design is often
the most legible typography, especially for screen display. Main titling may be centered, but a stronger composition is made when the main titles are aligned flush
left with the left side of the data area rectangle. The
number of digits in the scales along the axes should be
kept to a minimum so that data values can be easily
understood. Avoid the use of labeling boxes or leader
lines to identify the data lines, because the chart can become too cluttered.

Figure 5.4 Bar Chart

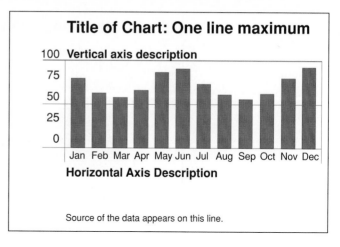

Figure 5.5 Grouped
Bar Chart

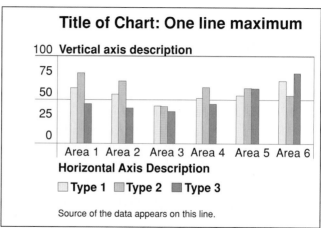

Bar Charts

Bar charts, such as the one pictured in Fig. 5.4, show
the data values with thick lines or bars that emphasize
the magnitude or size of the data values. (Sometimes
vertical bar charts are called column charts.) The bars
can be grouped as in Fig. 5.5, divided as in Fig. 5.6, op-
posed, or combined into 100 percent bars as in Fig. 5.7.
Bar charts are interchangeable with arithmetic line
charts and are just as easily understood by professional
and lay audiences. Bar charts differ in not being as
suitable as line charts for showing trends; they are better for emphasizing the actual values or differences between positive and negative values.

Figure 5.6 Divided
Bar Chart

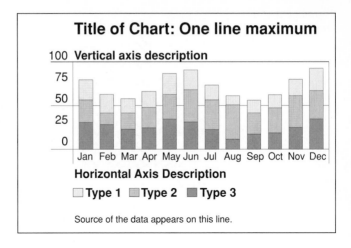

Figure 5.7 100 Percent
Bar Chart

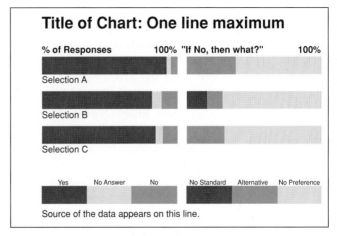

Many graphic design issues for bar charts are similar to those for line charts, particularly with respect to line weights, typography, and tick marks. If data values must appear near the end of the bars, the characters should be relatively small; otherwise, they will clutter up the ends of the bars and make the pattern of bars hard to read. The space between bars should be half the width of the bars or less; in fact, the space can even be omitted in some situations. For divided bar charts, select textures and colors that do not cause optical illusions or unnecessarily emphasize one segment in comparison to others. Pictured in Fig. 5.8 is a common error. The bars appear crooked because opposing diagonal-line patterns are used for the segments of the

Figure 5.8 Bar Chart
Illusion

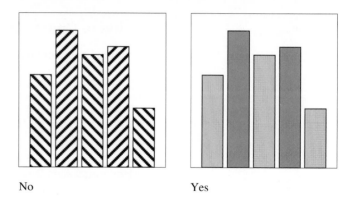

No   Yes

bar chart. If multiple bars are used, there should not be
more than three in a group.

Circle Charts

In the business world, the circle chart, also called a
pie chart, is as American as apple pie. This chart (see
Fig. 5.9) is similar to the 100 percent bar chart in showing the interrelation of components to a whole. Although it continues to be a popular method for showing
data, many chart-making guidebooks discourage the
use of circle charts because it is hard for readers to
compare areas accurately within one chart or among
several charts.

Designing circle charts is somewhat complex because
of the circular central shape. Main titling should be
centered over or under the circle if there are no other
layout constraints; however, titling can also appear
flush left with the left edge of the circle or even further
to the left to accommodate labels. Unless the sector
label typography is small, sector labels should be
placed outside of the sectors. All groups of labels
should be laid out in a simple arrangement. Leader
lines may be necessary to point to small sectors, but
they should not be oriented in many different angles.
In general, circle charts should use seven sectors or
less, and the sectors should not take up less than 5 percent (18 degrees) of the circle. Textures or colors selected for the sectors should not emphasize one over
another unless it is intended.

Figure 5.9 Circle Chart

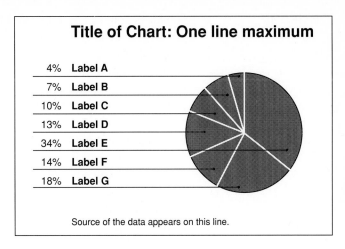

Title of Chart: One line maximum

4%	Label A
7%	Label B
10%	Label C
13%	Label D
34%	Label E
14%	Label F
18%	Label G

Source of the data appears on this line.

General Principles

Simplicity, clarity, and consistency are important for good chart design. Extraneous text should be kept to a minimum; titling should be brief and to the point. One item often neglected is the source of the data. In a slide sequence, identification need appear only once at the beginning, but data sources should appear on every printed chart.

Texture, color and spatial qualities of the lines, bars, and circles often overwhelm the eye in computer-assisted charts. These qualities can sometimes actually mislead viewers studying the data values. Charts can be stylized provided they do not interfere with the primary communication. A "Las Vegas" approach often implies that the chart data is of relatively little importance.

An especially important design consideration is in what media a chart will appear. Charts are sometimes designed for one medium but later used in another. A chart made for a high-resolution color slide show may find its way, inappropriately, into a black-and-white re-production in a report or into a lower-resolution video display. The proportions of the format, the typographic sizes, the amount of labeling, and especially the texture and color relationships need to be reconsidered. Some chart-making software and hardware products currently make poor automatic translations of displays for differ-ent output forms. The responsibility of good design is placed on the users.

Conclusion

Business graphics systems are putting increasingly sophisticated display possibilities into the hands of users who need to learn some of the basics of good chart design. The repertoire of chart forms is also enlarging, as project planning diagrams, star charts, and other kinds of displays find greater use.

One important point to remember is that few people really want to spend time designing charts. Most people are trying to solve a problem or make a point and would be pleased to have an inexpensive, efficient assistant make the display decisions for them, especially if many displays are necessary. In the near future, we shall see the emergence of systems with some "artificial graphic intelligence" that know how to lay out charts well, how to account for the needs of the data, and how to adjust the charts for different display environments.

In our own firm, as we design unique charts and templates for chart making, we are aware that it is impossible, even for computer-assisted graphic designers, to meet all the chart-making needs of the business world. Until many of the basic rules for good design can be imbedded in software and eventually in chips of silicon, it will be necessary for users to learn some of the basics. The following section and Bibliography Section 5.1 will help you find out more about chart making.

5.2 An Annotated Bibliography of Chart and Diagram Design

Introduction

Contemporary workstations offer developers and users the opportunity to display data, information, and knowledge in sophisticated visual layouts of charts and diagrams. Examples of charts and diagrams in user-interface design and electronic publishing design can be found in process or status depictions, training manuals, business graphics presentations, and reports. Developers and users will need to make sophisticated decisions about the design of these graphics, including typographic font selection, layout, illustration, color palette, symbols and pictograms, animation, and sequencing.

Traditionally, professional graphic designers made these decisions; now the responsibility often falls upon the developer or user of computer graphics systems. In most cases, the software can not automatically select the right kind of chart or diagram and then lay it out properly. In a few cases, clip-art or template libraries exist for a limited variety of charts and diagrams. In most cases, however, the quality of the final design still rests with the experience, imagination, and skill of the developer or user. Luckily, there are a number of references that provide excellent advice on issues, principles, recommendations, and case studies for what to do in designing charts and diagrams.

The references presented here have been chosen because they present their content well both in a verbal and visual form, and because most of them are available in art and design bookstores or from distributors. Sources for many of these references are identified in Section 1.3. Equipped with the background that these books provide programmers, managers, writers, editors, secretaries, researchers, that is, all those suddenly involved with developing and using information graphics on CRTs, on slide screens, and in publications, can make better decisions about complex chart and diagram design and produce higher visual quality in terms of communication effectiveness.

Recommended Publications

Auger, B.Y., *How to Run Better Business Meetings,* 3M Company, St. Paul., 1979, 214 pp. Although not strictly about chart and diagram design, this "executive guide to meetings that get things done" provides a chapter and an appendix on chart design. Of special interest is the explanation and analysis of the context in which these visual presentations are used.

Bertin, Jacques, *Semiology of Graphics,* trans. William J. Berg, The University of Wisconsin Press, Madison, 1983, 415 pp. Bertin presents a thorough analysis of graphic sign systems, the rules for design, and practical applications. Many unusual charts and diagrams are illustrated, primarily in black-and-white.

Carlsen, Robert D., and Donald L. Vest, *Encyclopedia of Business Charts,* Prentice-Hall, Inc., Englewood Cliffs, NJ, 1977, 886 pp. This unusual reference compendium shows more than 700 full-page black-and-white examples of more than 15 categories of charts, including scheduling, technical performance, quality control, and facilities.

Chambers, John, M., et al., *Graphical Methods for Data Analysis,* Wadsworth Statistics/Probability Series, Wadsworth International Group, Belmont, CA, 1983, 395 pp. This book surveys traditional and computer-oriented graphical methods for analyzing data, rather than communicating through charts and diagrams. While oriented to a technical audience, some of the presentation forms may be used for general audiences as well.

The Diagram Group, *Visual Comparisons,* St. Martin's Press, New York, 1980, 240 pp. The authors, specialists in presenting information in visual form, present an ingenious visual thesaurus depicting the relative speed, size, strength, etc. of animals, environmental and technological objects, astronomical bodies, etc. Comparisons of systems of numbers, geometry, and time-space measurements are provided as well. The material appears in unique layouts of charts and diagrams.

Heller, Steven, and Philip B. Meggs, *Graphic Design USA: 7,* The Annual of the American Institute of Graphic Arts, Watson-Guptil Publications, New York, 1986, pp. 248-319. The annual presents a view of a competition and exhibit of functional graphics that emphasizes well-designed charts and diagrams.

Herdeg, Walter, ed., *Graphis Diagrams,* Graphis Press, Zurich, 1981, 207 pp. This compilation of worldwide examples shows approximately 400 full-color illustrations of seven categories of charts and diagrams designed by graphic designers.

Holmes, Nigel, *Designer's Guide to Creating Charts and Diagrams,* Watson-Guptill Publications, 1984, 192 pp. This book might be more aptly entitled *Illustrator's Guide.* The author provides a news-magazine art director's perspective on how to add visual emphasis to charts and diagrams intended for mass publications to general audiences.

Huff, Darrell, *How to Lie with Statistics,* W.W. Norton and Co., New York, 1951, 142 pp. This small, classic paperback volume examines the dangers of presenting data in misleading verbal and visual formats. While primarily oriented to verbal texts, much of the analysis can be applied to visual presentations.

Japan Creators' Association, ed., *Diagraphics,* Japan Creators' Association Press, Tokyo, 1986, 304 pp. This compilation of worldwide examples shows more than 700 full-color illustrations of 13 categories of charts and diagrams designed by graphic designers.

Lockwood, Arthur, *Diagrams,* Watson-Guptill Publications, New York, 1969 (out of print), 144 pp. The author presents hundreds of examples, primarily black-and-white, of 24 categories of charts and diagrams. He also presents advice on design of these graphics.

MacGregor, A.J., *Graphics Simplified,* University of Toronto Press, Toronto, 1979, 64 pp. This slender volume presents an admirable summary of basic chart groups and essential design guidelines. It is an excellent introduction to the subject.

Martin, James, and Carma McClure, *Diagramming Techniques for Analysts and Programmers,* Prentice-Hall, Inc., Englewood Cliffs, NJ, 1985, 396 pp. This unusual volume explains the purpose, functions, and appearance of state and process diagrams suitable for depicting such contents as nested structures, data flows, state-transition diagrams, and decision trees.

Meilach, Donna Z., *Dynamics of Presentation Graphics,* Dow Jones-Irwin, Homewood, IL, 1986, 259 pp. Meilach surveys the basic needs for business graphics and presents illustrated techniques (many in color) for accomplishing them with current hardware and software products. Appendixes include sources for products as well as references to publications and organization.

Meyers, Cecil H., *Handbook of Basic Graphs: A Modern Approach,* Wadsworth International Group, Belmont, CA, 1970 (out of print), 214 pp. The author presents a lucid, well-organized explanation of a limited selection of charts with detailed design guidelines oriented to restrained use of typography, line elements, etc.

Schmid, Calvin F., and Standon E. Schmid, *Handbook of Graphic Presentation,* 2d ed., John Wiley and Sons, New York, 1979, 308 pp. The authors present a classic explanation of design techniques for general and technical charts oriented to technical audiences.

Tufte, Edward R., *Envisioning Information,* Graphics Press, Cheshire, CT, 1990, 200 pp. The author presents a second collection of data-presentation history, techniques, and recommendations.

—— *The Visual Display of Quantitative Information,* Graphics Press, Cheshire, CT, 1983, 197 pp. The author presents his theory of communicating data effectively in graphic form and examines historical as well as contemporary examples to demonstrate his points.

Tukey, John, W., *Exploratory Data Analysis,* Addison-Wesley Publishing Co., Inc., Reading, MA, 1977, 688 pp. Tukey's classic text on quantitative methods of data analysis concentrates on understanding the implications of data and determining effective ways to describe the deeper meanings of the data. Tukey introduces some unique means for presenting relationships in specialized chart design. The book is technical and full of mathematical case studies.

White, Jan V., *Using Charts and Graphs,* R. R. Bowker Co., New York, 1984, 202 pp. The author surveys the basic kinds of charts and diagrams, examines communication goals, and presents practical suggestions for variation and combination in many black-and-white illustrations.

5.3 An Annotated Bibliography of Map Design

Introduction

Many recent publications focus on availability of cartographic database display on personal computers as well as on high-end specialized workstations. Increasingly, maps are found in executive reports, training manuals, business graphics slide presentations, decision support systems, CAD/CAM applications, vehicle-navigation systems, and electronic publishing of all kinds. Maps are used as an archival tool for long-term storage and retrieval of information, as well as for rapid decision making. The increased use of maps in computer graphics systems creates the need for effective display of geographical information to the general public and to professionals who are graphically editing or viewing the contents of these cartographic images. Developers and users will need to make the sophisticated design decisions that professional cartographers and graphic designers traditionally have made.

There are a number of references that provide excellent advice on issues, principles, recommendations, and examples of fine map design to guide the neophyte. Some are now quite old, but they are still relevant to the needs of people trying to get the best visual-communication quality out of computer graphics systems. Major atlases, published by such firms as the *New York Times,* are not included as they are readily available in most bookstores. Professional journals of cartography are not included also because they are available in most large libraries. As map design includes complex decisions about typography, color, and symbolism, Sections 2.3, 3.4, and 4.2 are also of interest.

Recommended Publications

Albers, Josef, *Interaction of Color*, Yale University Press, New Haven, 1975, 81 pp. The author, a noted artist and teacher, presents his analysis of color interaction and composition phenomena in a classic, illustrated text for art and design students that is also relevant to map designers.

Anderson, Robert, Robert Helms, and Norman Z. Shapiro, "Design Considerations for Computer-Based Interactive Map Display Systems," report no. R-2382-ARPA, prepared for DARPA by the Rand Corporation, Santa Monica, CA, February 1979, 45 pp. Although dated, this prescient report explains lucidly the uses of interactive maps and presents design considerations for their effective display.

Artscanada, no. 188/189 Spring 1974, 106 pp. This special issue on maps and mapping, including an article by John Warkentin, "Discovering the Shape of Canada," includes provocative text and illustrations about the nature of maps from an aesthetic as well as functional point of view.

Bertin, Jacques, *Semiology of Graphics*, trans. William J. Berg, The University of Wisconsin Press, Madison, 1983, ISBN 0-299-09060-4, 415 pp. Bertin's classic analysis of graphic sign systems presents useful information on visual coding techniques and a major chapter on maps.

Brown, Lloyd A., *The Story of Maps*, Dover Publications, New York, 1977, ISBN 0-486-23873-3, 397 pp. This historical survey uses 86 monochrome illustrations to trace the development of map forms.

Gould, Peter, and Rodney White, *Mental Maps*, Penguin Books, Baltimore, 1974, 204 pp. The authors introduce the concept of geography of perception, the interior images we form of places, and examine their role in decision making.

Guelke, Leonard, ed., "The Nature of Cartographic Communication," Monograph no. 19, Supplement no. 1 to *Canadian Cartographer* 14, 1977, 147 pp, published by B.V. Gutsell, Department of Geography, York University, Toronto, Canada. This academic monograph presents some thoughts on the nature of cartographic information and how to present that information well.

Harvey, P.D.A., *The History of Topographical Maps*, Thames and Hudson, 1980, LC 80-80086, 199 pp. This survey, illustrated with 116 figures (10 in color), shows the development of a specific kind of map that uses symbols and pictures to provide terrain information.

Herdeg, Walter, ed., *Graphis Diagrams*, Graphis Press, Zurich, 1981, ISBN 3-85709-410-9, 207 pp. The book is a worldwide visual synopsis of well-designed images and devotes a chapter to cartographic diagrams and decorative maps.

Hooper, Kristina, "Experiential Mapping," no. R-3478-ARPA, DARPA, Arlington, VA, 1981, 276 pp. This publication was produced with a companion videodisk. The report examines new techniques and design approaches for the display of map information, including environmental simulation, representation of objects, and spatial layout.

Lockwood, Arthur, *Diagrams*, Watson-Guptill Publications, New York, 1969, British ISBN 289-37030-2, 144 pp. This visual survey of charts, maps, and diagrams for the graphic designer includes a specific chapter on explanatory and statistical map design.

"Map Data Catalog," U.S. Department of the Interior, National Cartographic Information Center National Mapping Program, Washington. This well-designed (but poorly identified) publication presents visual examples of kinds of maps, their uses, and the availability of certain maps through the NCIC.

"Maps of the World's Nations," Vol 1: Western Hemisphere, no. 041-00078-1, Central Intelligence Agency, Washington, January 1976, 46 pp. This volume, and others in the series, show clear, well-designed examples of brief atlases. The color is subtle, the typography simple and very legible.

Muehrcke, Philip, "Thematic Cartography," Resource paper no. 19, Assoc. of American Geographers, Washington, 1972, LC 72-77214, 66 pp. This college monograph succinctly provides an explanation of thematic cartography and computer-based applications. The images are out of date, but not the fundamental concepts.

"Process Color Guide," 2d ed., S.D. Scott Printing Co., New York, 1986, 96 pp., large format. A high-quality printing company presents almost 5000 two- and three-color process ink mixtures.

Peucker, Thomas K. "Computer Cartography," Resource paper no. 17, Assoc. of American Geographers, Washington, 1972, LC 72-75261, 75 pp. This college monograph is an introduction to computer data capture, management, and display. Many of the images are outdated, but not the essential concepts.

Robinson, Arthur H., and Barbara Bartz Petchenik, *The Nature of Maps*, University of Chicago Press, Chicago, 1976, ISBN 0-226-72281-3, 138 pp. In a small-format monograph, Robinson, one of the leading American cartographers, and his coauthor provide a succinct, powerful essay on the visual language of maps and their meaning.

Robinson Arthur, Randall Sale, and Joel Morrison, *Elements of Cartography*, John Wiley and Sons, New York, 1978, ISBN 0-471-01781-7, 448 pp. Robinson, one of the leading American cartographers, and his cowriters present a very readable, highly recommended complete survey of mapping concepts, techniques, and design principles.

Weltman, Gershon, "Maps: A Guide to Innovative Design," Report no. PTR-1033S-78-1, prepared for DARPA by Perceptronics, Woodland Hills, CA, February 1979, 249 pp. This forward-looking research report examines maps and their uses, the mapping processes, map design examples, and computer-based applications to the mapping process. Although dated, it contains valuable discussion of issues and essential concepts.

Conclusion

The availability of relatively inexpensive cartographic databases, display systems, and color hardcopy devices coincides with an increasing need for maps by marketing and research staffs. The general public also has a need for and interest in maps. Improvements in the means for cartographically communicating facts, concepts, and emotions to persuade, inform, and aesthetically please the reader/viewer is a major challenge for contemporary map design.

This publication list provides a starting point for analysis, planning, design, and production of cartographic displays. Sources for many of these references are identified in Section 1.3. Equipped with the background that these publications provide, programmers, managers, writers, editors, secretaries, researchers, that is, all those suddenly involved with developing and using information graphics on CRTs, on slide screens, and in publications, can make better decisions about designing maps and produce higher visual quality in terms of communication effectiveness.

Chapter 6 Screen Design for User Interfaces

User interfaces provide an outstanding challenge to use visible language well. In addition to the attributes of the printed page or slides and overheads, screen design provides an opportunity for interaction design as well. Every element is potentially changeable in its shape, location, color, texture, size, etc. Designing screens includes the design of windows, menus, icons, cursors, dialogue boxes, and control panels. Orchestrating the design of these components is a supreme test for systematic, information-oriented graphic designs.

6.1 Common User-Interface Design

Introduction

From academic journals to commercial publications, one topic that seems to be of increasing interest to both vendors and users is the user interface. Recently, several companies have announced major software development projects that help to establish productwide, companywide, and even industrywide standards for user-interface design. Some products provide the ability to affect the overall appearance and interaction capabilities of a user interface, while others focus primarily upon window management and more limited control of input and output changes. Some companies provide sophisticated user-interface management systems (UIMS) in which a variety of applications and input/output devices can be attached to a core of software that facilitates communication between the user's actions and the application. Among the window-management software in the news recently are Presentation Manager, OPEN

LOOK, X Windows, DECWindows, and Microsoft
Windows. Some products like Easel, NeXT's
NextStep, and Hewlett Packard's NewWave have the
potential to permit a user to customize user interfaces.
One possible goal for these systems, tools, and techniques is to create a common user interface across
products.

**Definition of a
Common
User Interface**

A common user interface is a set of rules used
across a group of products that formally specifies the
visual presentation of data and functions, the user's interaction, and the logical organization and behavior of
information. The various products coming into the market place make it easier to create a user interface, but
they also make it easier to assemble a poor user interface more quickly than ever before. Well-designed user
interfaces must account for the following key
components:

• Easily grasped metaphor and idea or image that cap-
tures the essence of the system

• Appropriate organization of data, functions, tools,
roles, and people in a task-oriented cognitive model

• Efficient navigation schema in the cognitive model,
that is, the action relationships that enable reading and
writing of these data, functions, tools, roles, and people

• Quality appearance characteristics (the size, shape, col-
or, orientation, location, etc.) of each visual element on
the screen

• Effective interaction sequencing (the logical protocols
for the visual elements) and their relation to hardware
input/output devices

In addition, invariably important factors in establishing a common user interface are these:

- Product and user groups that may limit innovation

- Special requirements of international customers

- User-interface concerns of corpo ᛫ user groups

- Available UIMS and computer-platform constraints

- Strong product identity different from the competition

- Tool sets

- Customizability for end users

- Screen metaphor

- Advanced graphical editing and window management

- Help/online documentation

- Documentation, training, and marketing requirements

- Demonstrations of the product

**Benefits of
a Common
User-Interface
Approach**

There are many benefits to implementing a common user-interface design approach.

Production: Consistent components are easier to assemble, maintain, and reuse, thereby creating cost savings. One study at Kodak estimated a development cost break-even point at four products based on a 20 percent code savings through reuse of code.

Marketing: Customers recognize a family of products; selling a recognized product name and appearance is usually easy.

Learning: Users become familiar with simple, clear, and consistent functions and features quickly.

Use: Users become more proficient through familiar, well-designed techniques; they can then focus on unique aspects of their tasks.

Service: Documentation and training become simpler, and more consistent.

Legal: Proprietary components of the user interface maybe easier to protect if they are consistently embodied in a product and its documentation.

Technical: A consistent approach makes it easier to conform with international standards, such as the draft standard on color display for CRT screens that the ISO currently circulating.

Quality: Clear standards make product quality assessment easier and more reliable.

A Prototype Case Study

Some window-management systems provide such a diversity of detailing in parts that it may be hard to imagine what the whole will be. It is useful to look at a complete approach to understand the level of work required to accomplish a common user-interface design. One example is a prototype approach developed at Kodak. Figures 6.1 and 6.2 show two typical examples from one product released using a design developed by Dan Rosenberg and Walter Bubie of Kodak, Joy Underhill of Underhill Associates, and our firm.

Overview

Eastman Kodak Company developed a comprehensive prototype user-interface design for computer-based image- and text-processing systems. The design was intended for large displays (19 to 21 inches) with resolutions of 80 pixels per inch or greater. The Image Editing Workstation was the first announced product to use this design. This product was used for high-resolution image editing in the fields of remote sensing, cartography, and earth resource management. The project was the cooperative effort of human factors, graphic design, industrial design, and software engineering. These groups developed an innovative design goal: to standardize the "look and feel" of computer products and promote corporate image guidelines via carefully designed screen components.

The resulting common user-interface design introduced computer software into two new areas: product-form definition and corporate-image promotion. In this project, product form was not defined solely by the physical container that housed a product; it also included the software used to display and interact with computer screens. The CUI included the following components. (See Fig. 6.1 and 6.2):

Desktop Background: All visual elements appear on a screen "desktop," depicted in neutral gray of approximately 50 percent value.

Help Bar: The help bar displays dynamic one-line help as the cursor moves, and can be expanded to a full-size help window.

Icons: Three kinds of icons are used: desktop, place, and global.

The desktop icon and its resulting menu allow users to alter global system characteristics, change the place icons displayed at the top of the screen, and enter text in non-Roman languages. Global icons, such as help, undo, and exit, complete the same function in all windows.

Mouse Bar: This area is segmented to correspond to the number of mouse buttons. As the mouse moves, the meaning of each button is displayed here.

Windows: One or more windows may result when a place icon is chosen to allow the user to work within a software application. Place icons represent software applications and typically open one or more windows.

Product Title Bar: This element, borrowed form Kodak's corporate-communications layout standards, is

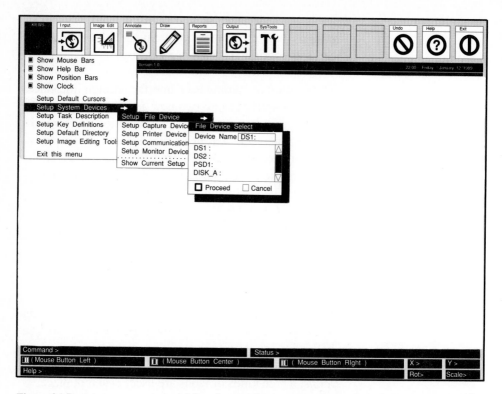

Figure 6.1 Prototype
Common User Interface:
Use of Desktop Icon

used for the product name, time, date, user name, product version, and other systemwide information.

Status Bar: This area displays informational messages.

Command Bar: This area allows users to type in commands to be applied to the contents of a window and enter text in non-Roman languages, such as Japanese.

Window Title Bar: This area is used to display the application name and two window buttons, and to move the window to a new location.

Control Panels: These areas are used to manipulate appearance, interaction, or information organization. For example, in graphics applications, control panels help the user manipulate graphic elements (such as drawing a box or shading the background of a drawing).

Figure 6.2 Prototype
Common User Interface:
Use of a Control Panel

Window Buttons (optional): Four "buttons" at each corner of a window permit activities such as shuffling windows (much like a stack of papers), resizing windows,
and closing windows.

Scroll Bars (optional): These areas are used to shift the
view of the window contents.

Actions: This row of boxes represents the major
function a user can perform on the information in a
window. Selecting an action may result in further
prompting, a menu, or another window.

Prompt Boxes: These areas are used to solicit additional information from users.

Figure 6.1 Shows some typical elements, such as a
product title bar derived from corporate graphics standards; use of standard bars for commands, status,
mouse-button meanings, and help; icons or symbols

along the top to represent applications; and standard symbols at the top right to represent undo, help, and exit functions available in all windows.

Figure 6.2 shows typical window title bars, action bars, control panels, and prompt boxes that change their contents according to the particular data and navigation needs. The position and size of most components is governed by an underlying spatial grid for the default layout of the screen that uses a title bar's height as a basic measuring unit. Detailed specifications cover the precise manner in which all typographic, symbolic, and image elements appear. These details are contained in a lengthy common user-interface specification document.

Unique interaction techniques include assigning generic meanings for the three-button mouse when applied to the global undo, help, and exit icons. Respectively, the left, middle, and right buttons mean a little, more, and most intense action is required.

Conclusion

The Kodak approach is only one of many paradigms being developed in the laboratory and available in commercial product releases. In the next few years the computer industry will settle upon the most successful of these approaches for the benefit of both the producers and the consumers of user interfaces. Already, we see the need of establishing well-designed templates for the tool kits being built so that most users will not need to make the many decisions necessary to put together superior user interfaces. A common user-interface approach points the way to increased ease of production and higher quality, but not without attention to the design of each element as well as the total composition. As with almost all aspects of computer graphics, good design must be a factor in achieving good communication.

6.2 The User-Interface Standards Manual as a Tool for Effective Management

Introduction

User-interface design is a complex task requiring in-process documentation that programmers, research and development managers, and marketing staff can consult. A user-interface standards manual meets their needs for information by providing a detailed specification for screen appearance and user-computer interaction. The contents of such as document need to be organized carefully and completed in cycles corresponding to the planning, design, and implementation schedule of a computer graphics system. This section explains the typical components of a user-interface manual as a tool for effective management in product development.

For almost any serious computer graphics system, creating the user interface is often a complicated task involving several staff members who must describe and explain the systems's functional capabilities, screen appearance, and user interaction. As plans for software and hardware evolve, theories on appearance and interaction change. In order to document and control these changes, a special medium is required that embodies the current conventions or standards together with historical information (to trace versions and responsibility for decision making) and supplementary technical information.

Several publications have appeared (see Bibliography, Section 6.2, McCormick and Bleser 1985 and Brown 1986) that present guidelines and recommendations for user-interface design. The User-interface Standards Manual (UISM) is a precise specification for a particular system that employs the wisdom of general sources of information and relates it to particular circumstances. The UISM is similar to graphic design standards manuals prepared for large corporate firms, environmental signage systems, and mass transportation environments. As with these other manuals, the UISM must elaborate on the user population, the characteristics of the system, and the means for production or fabrication.

Our firm has developed the contents and organization of UISMs and have used them in our consulting for such firms and organizations as Commodore-Amiga, Federal Express, Lawrence Berkeley Laboratory, Motorola, NCR, Pacific Bell, Ricoh, Reuters, Scitex, 3M, and DARPA. Yet, the art of user-interface design is still too young to be called a science. I do not claim that the organization and contents of a UISM is definitive, but that the approach presents a reasonable and demonstrably useful alternative to other formulations.

Purpose of the UISM

The UISM represents a taxonomy of the elements of components of the user interface, principles or rules for effective appearance and interaction, depictions of the elements, and examples of components. Because the design of a user interface can be as complicated as the design of a building, it is necessary to have clear blueprints or plans for the construction of the system. In fact, one can speak of creating the architecture of information in designing a user interface together with the databases that support it.

The purpose of the UISM is to facilitate the process of building the user interface, from concept to diagram, design, and implementation. The UISM is, in a sense, never finished because it is continually being updated.

What is a UISM and Who Needs It?

The UISM is organized according to concepts derived from the theory of semiotics, (see Bibliography, Section 6.2, Eco 1976). As noted in Sections 3.1 and 3.2, semiotics defines signs as icons (representational), indexes (related by cause and effect), and symbols (abstract or conventional). Semiotics also defines four dimensions of sign relationship: lexical, syntactic, semantic, and pragmatic. The lexical dimension refers to production of signs. Syntactics refers to the relationship of signs to each other, for example, an element may be larger or redder than another. Semantics refers to the relationship between signs and their referents, for example, an element may denote 'stop' or 'printer.' Pragmatics refers to the relationship between the sign and the persons who use or consume it; for example, an element may be too difficult to read for color-blind males at a distance of 60 centimeters.

The UISM is structured to reflect these dimensions of semiotics. Within these areas, the contents presents a summary of relevant principles derived from human factors, information-oriented graphic design, computer science, applied psychology, and other disciplines. Examples appear to clarify this content. Specifications provide details on how to produce and implement the various components of the user interface.

Who are the users of the UISM? These include programmers and managers of research and development who are the primary contributors to and maintainers of the UISM document. However, the UISM is also of value to marketing staff who wish to understand what the proposed system will do, how it will accomplish its functions, and for whom the system is intended. Marketing may wish to contribute ideas or check up on facets affecting their own plans. Even end users or third parties interested in consistent future enhancements will wish to consult the UISM in order to maintain conceptual and perceptual continuity with the current system.

Initially, the UISM must characterize the major components of the computer graphics system and its environment of use: users, the functions or tools from the user's point of view, hardware, the interface, software, and data. In describing the tools and data, the UISM must characterize precisely what global information is available from business, financial, political, social, or technical spheres, what management information resides in the system, and information about the users themselves. This material is then used in the later portions of the manual involving lexical, syntactic, semantics, and pragmatics specifications.

Lexical Issues

Production would consider capabilities for providing hardware, software, and suitable databases for the system. Device/task and hardware tradeoffs would be included in this section. Delivery would consider installation issues: activities, competing activities, the physical environment, backup facilities, maintenance, etc.

Syntactics Issues

The syntactics section of the UISM presents a taxonomy of elements of appearance and interaction together with their depictions and implementation. Elements of appearance include spatial layout of the screen, treatment of windows, typography, nontypographic signs, color, display enhancements, sequencing, and animation. Hardcopy considerations are also relevant, particularly with respect to visual consistency between screen and paper, film, or videotape. Elements of interaction include tasks, techniques, and styles.

Spatial layout concerns the screen format, its size and proportion. Of particular importance is the establishment of spatial grids that govern the location of screen command/control and status indicator metadata (titles, labels, footnotes, marginalia, headers, etc.) and data itself.

Windows must be described for single and multiwindow environments. The UISM must present any menus or indexes of commands and contents and any subwindows that contain video display, messages (errors, alerts, etc.) and online assistance.

The UISM gives particular attention to typography. Typical matters of font selection, resolution, screen to paper correspondence, and issues of eligibility and readability are described. Conventions of titling, field labels, tabular numerical data, prose text (which may consist of main text, footnotes, captions, etc.), and punctuation are also relevant.

The nontypographic signs includes cursors, icons, visual indicators of process and state, maps, charts, diagrams, and pictorial imagery that may be generated by the computer or come from scanned video sources. Each of these items requires detailed description and explanation.

The color discussion can include psychological and human-factors issues, cultural or ritualistic cues, aesthetic issues, general coding schemes, corporate-identity aspects, and specific data portrayal codes.

Display enhancements would include discussion of highlighting or lowlighting, temporal highlighting (blinking), and sound cueing.

Sequencing and animation cover the primary space and motion metaphors of the user interface. Some systems are planar, having only one large window within which all information is displayed. Other systems use an approach in which the user pops through a set of planes to reach the planes "below." A third approach, currently in vogue, is to use multiple planes or windows piled up on top of the lowest or primary plane.

Interaction tasks described in the UISM include the basic functions of selecting/picking, entering data, reviewing data, manipulating data, annotating, and changing the display parameters. UISM must detail how the user enters the display, moves within it, moves between screens or windows, and concludes a sequence of moves. Of special importance is scrolling and zooming, how the user moves sideways, up and down, and forward or backward in a display. Each of these movements may be perceptual or conceptual. In conceptual movements, the user changes levels, from main windows or menus to sublevels of these entities.

Techniques of interaction refer to the physical means of accomplishing tasks given the characteristics of input and display devices. The details of technique may be carried to as deep a level of computer-based explication as necessary. At the lowest levels the UISM passes from visible language to computer language programming. Actions described in this section include command entry, question and answer, form fill-in, menu selection, graphic interaction, document entry. Input devices may include touch, keyboard, mouse or puck, tablet, and voice. The UISM details not only the input stimulus but the elaborations of response.

Styles of interaction concern conventions imposed by the operating system; conventions involving the use of icons or symbols as a means of selection; conventions established for frame to frame movement, for example, from standard introductory displays to texts, to tables, to charts; and conventions for menu selection style (global, local, imbedded, explicit). The selection of styles may be optional or predetermined, variable or constant, and standard or nonstandard in their operation. Of special importance are the means of accelerating interaction for experts (shortcuts) and the blocking of interaction for security reasons.

Semantic Issues

The UISM also explains the concepts denoted by the syntactic elements of the user interface. Here the UISM would ask, what do the parts of the display mean? what are they signifying? The taxonomical index of displays (screens), words, colors, and actions is discussed in this section.

The index of displays must list all major kinds of screens, such as, titles, indexes, pictorial, chart, diagram, tabular, and text. Each of these displays may have varying levels of abstraction, of density of data portrayal, and of data portrayed including current status, trend over time, etc. This index must also describe the significance of the parts of typical screens, such as title bars, icons, and information-display areas. Finally, the relationship of levels of information from screen to screen must be presented.

The index of words explains the categories and characteristics of all conventional text elements. The choice, order, and synonyms for control words must be clarified. Control words include commands, titles, indexes, legends, footnotes, special messages, etc. Standard and nonstandard acronyms and abbreviations must be listed. Titling hierarchy should be included. Messages such as those for errors, alerts, and assistance must also be described and explained. It may be necessary to include an appendix specifically devoted to jargon of the particular user group or data.

The index of color depicts the coding for elements of structure and process, status, evaluated data, unevaluated data, unavailable entities, not-applicable entities etc.

The index of actions links the functions and features to the tools understood by the user. The meanings for selection, annotation, review, etc. are explained in this index. The user interface must account for limitations of hardware, software, budget, time, and human resources. It must also account for the limitations of the human users.

Pragmatic Issues

Planning covers analysis of the total product situation: needs, expectations, human-factors considerations, and the objectives of the proposed system. Needs might include those for data manipulation, communication, data entry, data access, and decision support. Human-factors issues might involve screen resolution, color sensitivity and color-deficient viewing, legibility of characters, and temporal sequencing limitations.

The consumption subsection describes the user population's skill and experience levels, their frequency of use, and other relevant characteristics. Also detailed are matters of user guidance, training, and support. Technical support for the users and maintainers of the system must also be indicated. Finally, the security entry, manipulation, and access conditions must be presented.

Appendixes

The UISM's appendixes provide supplementary information needed by development and marketing staff. One component covers the maintenance of the UISM itself.

Typical Table of Contents

Following up on the above recommendations, a generic table of contents might consist of the following:

Introduction
    Purpose of the UISM
        Taxonomy classification
        Explanation of the
        Evolution of the as a living document
    What is the UISM
        Organization
        Content
    Who will use the
        Programmers
        End users
        Managers
        Support staff
        Research and development staff
        Marketing staff
    How to use the UISM
        Production
        System use
        Maintenance
        Marketing
    Description of the user's environment
        Hardware
        Software
        Content
    Lexical structure
        Appearance
        Verbal
        Acoustic
        Interaction
    Syntactical structure
        Elements of appearance
            Spatial layout
            Windows
            Typography
            Non-typographic signs
            Color
            Display enhancements
            Animation
            Sequencing

Elements of interaction
    Tasks of interaction
    Techniques
    Styles of interaction
    Selection of technique/style
    Accelerated paths of interaction (shortcuts)
    Security
  Hardcopy
Semantics
  Elements of display
    Kinds of screens
    Parts of a screen
    Attributes
    Relationships
Elements of words
  Control words
  Acronyms and abbreviations
  Titling hierarchy
  Messages
Elements of color
  Evaluated/unevaluated data
  Command and control
  Status
Elements of actions
  Selection
  Annotation
  Display sequencing
Pragmatics
  Planning
    Situation analysis
    User groups
  Production
    Capability
    Operating system and conventions
  Delivery
    Installation environment
    Device implication
  Consumption
    User population
    User guidance
    Global actions
    Custom features and adaptability

Conclusion   Currently UISMs are kept in a three-ring notebook because materials come from diverse (sometimes incom-
patible) computer-based and manual sources. In the
future, all textual and graphic elements will be stored in
a computer-based system. Ideally all contents of the
UISM would be contained in a relational database. This
would facilitate corrections, revisions, and tracking of
user-interface development. If inheritance properties
were accounted for, global revisions of the user interface under development would be facilitated. At such a
state, the computer graphics world would have an expert system facility for building and managing user interfaces. Such advanced, sophisticated, and general
purpose capabilities will not be available in the immediate future. In the meantime the paper-based UISM
provides a capable, efficient management tool for di-
recting and recording the successful development
of the user interface.

Chapter 7 A Comparison of Graphical User Interfaces

To assist designers of graphical user interfaces, this section details similarities and differences among six major graphical user-interface (GUI) products. This chapter addresses the functional capabilities and usability characteristics of the following windowing systems:

Apple Macintosh OS
NextStep
OPEN LOOK GUI
Microsoft Windows
OS/2 Presentation Manager
OSF/Motif Window Manager and Toolkit

The windowing system is similar to an operating system. Instead of file systems or CPU cycles, however, the windowing system manages resources such as screen space and input devices. In GUIs, the windowing system acts as a front end to the operating system by shielding the end-user from the abstract and often confusing syntax and vocabulary of a keyboard-oriented command language.

The following chapter is divided into four parts. Section 7.1 offers explanations of the selected windowing systems. Sections 7.2-7.7 describe the basic components of six windowing systems. These sections also provide comparative data in figures containing tables and screen images. Section 7.8 examines a number of frequently performed tasks in terms of the steps users must take to accomplish them in each of the six windowing systems.

137

Section 7.9 reviews the performance, configurability, and standardization of the windowing systems and closes with a brief summary that highlights the most important differences among the six products reviewed.

Additional detailed information describing the components of each system is presented in Appendixes A and B. The order in which the systems are described is the same for each section of the chapter so that information for a particular product can be located quickly. To facilitate cross-product comparisons while maintaining a consistent order of presentation, similar products such as Windows, Presentation Manager, and Motif are placed in adjacent positions in the sequence.

The Macintosh appears first because it is the oldest and most established of the windowing systems. For a large segment of the user population, the Macintosh defined the standard against which newer products must compete. NextStep is considered next because of its similarity to the Macintosh from the standpoint of its target user population and the level of complexity of the conceptual model presented by the GUI.

The OPEN LOOK GUI is similar to both NextStep and Motif. It appears third and is followed by Motif, which is grouped with Windows and Presentation Manager. This arrangement allows the two simple user model systems (Macintosh and NextStep), the three workstation class machines (NeXT, OPEN LOOK, Motif), and the three IBM-standard systems (Motif, Windows, Presentation Manager) to be grouped simultaneously. The same order of presentation used in the text is maintained in the column organization of the figures.

This chapter employs a single set of generic terminology to describe the components of the products being compared. Note that product references refer to the state of the products in early 1990.

7.1 Windowing Systems

Introduction

Each of the windowing systems discussed in this chapter has a unique place in the history of GUIs. Each system also has unique features, which are reviewed briefly in this section.

Macintosh

The Apple Macintosh was introduced in 1984 as the first mass-market computer featuring a high-resolution, bit-mapped graphic display and a direct manipulation interaction style. Its windowing system is built on top of a proprietary library of operating-system and user-interface toolkit routines in the Macintosh ROM.

The classic Macintosh is a single-tasking system with a high level of responsiveness and a very simple user model. Apple has succeeded in creating widespread acceptance among third-party software developers for their standard human-interface components. As a result, knowledge about familiar Macintosh applications can ease the task of learning new applications.

The Macintosh was the first computer system with a GUI to gain widespread market acceptance and experience significant commercial success. Its popularity, particularly in nontechnical market segments traditionally unreceptive toward computing, can be attributed in large part to Apple's commitment to the creation of a consistent and user-supportive human interface.

Because of its historical precedence and market penetration, the Macintosh has established the standard of interaction by which GUIs are judged. The degree of responsiveness to the actions of the user demonstrates the quality of interaction that is possible when the windowing system is integrated tightly with a particular hardware and software environment.

NextStep

The NextStep user interface provides a windowing system and graphical desktop environment for the NeXT Computer, which began shipping in 1988. The four component modules of the NextStep user interface are the Window Server, the Workspace Manager, the Application Kit, and the Interface Builder.

NextStep was the first in a series of products to adopt a simulated three-dimensional appearance for its standard components. The Window Server uses Display PostScript to create high-quality grayscale screen displays providing graphics that can be output on any PostScript printer.

The Application Kit provides a standard set of object-oriented components that can be customized by application developers. The Interface Builder is an end-user oriented tool that allows users to link these objects to system- and application-level functions with no additional programming. With this tool, standard OPEN LOOK human-interface components can be used to automate the user's tasks.

Like the Macintosh human interface, NextStep is oriented toward the needs of the nontechnical user. A straightforward conceptual model, a simple set of controls, and a well-developed collection of software tools shields the user from the complexity of the operating system and increases the suitability of the system for the initially targeted users (students and scholars) in higher education. Although the sophisticated UNIX-based operating system makes some degree of complexity inevitable, the design of the NextStep human interface makes the system accessible even for completely UNIX-naive users.

OPEN LOOK

The OPEN LOOK GUI was developed jointly by Sun Microsystems and AT&T as the standard operating environment for UNIX System V.4. The GUI exists as a layer on top of a base windowing system that provides the imaging-model and network-communication services. Versions of OPEN LOOK have been implemented on top of both the X Window System and Sun's Network-extensible Window System (NeWS).

Guidance for OPEN LOOK developers is provided by an exemplary functional specification and style guide. An explicit goal of the OPEN LOOK designers was to avoid potential legal challenges by creating innovative appearance and behavior characteristics. As a result, many of the conventions adopted deviate significantly from the industry norm.

A contrasting approach is adopted by OPEN LOOK. Its orientation toward maximum functionality is evident in the numerous context-sensitive and mode-specific operations it provides. While it, too, should make the UNIX world relatively accessible even for inexperienced users, the extended functionality of OPEN LOOK itself introduces an additional layer of complexity that is not seen in NextStep or the Macintosh human interface.

OSF/Motif

OSF/Motif is a window-manager and user-interface toolkit developed by DEC and Hewlett-Packard for the Open Software Foundation (OSF). Motif provides an alternative to OPEN LOOK that is linked to the OSF version of standard UNIX.

Like OPEN LOOK, the Motif Window Manager exists as a software layer atop the network-oriented X Window System. Appearance can be modified independently of the functional characteristics of the resulting system, and individual vendors are encouraged to customize the functional shell with their own proprietary widget sets.

The standard appearance and behavior of the Motif Window Manager are based on the OS/2 Presentation Manager. PC users familiar with that system or with Microsoft Windows will have little difficulty adapting to Motif on a workstation-level machine. Like NextStep, the Standard Motif widget set provides a simulated three-dimensional appearance.

OSF/Motif provides a GUI for a high-end, network-based computing environment whose appearance and behavior is consistent with that of Microsoft Windows and the OS/2 Presentation Manager. Because of their de facto standardization on IBM and compatible platforms, these operating environments are expected to predominate in the movement toward GUIs for PC-based systems. OSF anticipates that knowledge of Windows and the Presentation Manager will transfer easily to Motif, making it the windowing system of choice when PC users upgrade to workstation platforms.

The implementation of Motif on top of the network-transparent X Window System allows Motif to leverage an emerging standard in the workstation environment as well. Motif provides a windowing system that can serve as a bridge between the PC and workstation environments. Its potential for easing this transition will increase the attractiveness of Motif for organizations integrating high-performance workstations with existing PC networks.

Microsoft Windows and OS/2 Presentation Manager

Microsoft Windows was created in 1985 as a multi-tasking, graphics-oriented alternative to the character-based environment provided by MS-DOS on PC-compatible systems. The bit-mapped displays and mouse-driven menus provided by Windows first opened the door to graphics-oriented software on the PC.

Initially, Windows was limited by many of the design characteristics (640K address space, low-quality display, etc.) of the DOS environment on which it was built. Recent enhancements, however, have increased the responsiveness and graphical quality of Windows, particularly on 80386-based machines.

The OS/2 Presentation Manager was developed jointly by Microsoft and IBM in 1987 as the standard graphics-based end-user environment for the operating system replacing MS-DOS. Presentation Manager will become the standard operating environment for IBM and compatible microcomputers in the 1990s. The appearance and behavior of Presentation Manager are derived primarily from Windows, which will eventually provide an identical user model for users in the MS-DOS environment.

Microsoft Windows and the OS/2 Presentation Manager must satisfy a very different market consisting largely of existing MS-DOS users in business and technical environments. The extensive support for keyboard-based control provided by these products reflects the heritage of the character-based DOS interface, which has historically relied heavily on keystroke combinations for selecting from menus and dialogue boxes.

7.2 Windowing-System Overview

Introduction

Windowing systems divide the display screen into multiple functional areas that provide a means of monitoring and controlling multiple application programs or manipulating multiple data objects in a graphical environment. The windows in which documents and applications are presented provide a set of well-defined visual and functional contexts that allow multiple processes to time-share a single set of input devices (mouse, keyboard, etc.) and a limited amount of physical display space. The windowing code (software architecture, the method of window management, and the base window system's imaging model) can have noticeable effects on the quality of the displays and the level of interaction experienced by the user. These factors are described in this section.

Software Architecture

The location and organization of the code that implements the windowing system can influence the responsiveness, device dependence, and resource requirements of the resulting system. Kernel-based architectures, for example, provide high levels of interactivity but are dependent on the architecture and available resources of a single machine. Client-server architectures allow a single instance of the windowing system code to be shared across entire networks of heterogeneous machines, but response times may be limited by the communication bandwidth of the network.

Kernel-Based Architecture

In kernel-based systems, windowing services are provided by some portion of the operating system itself, or by a standard add-on module that resides along with the operating system in RAM- or ROM-based libraries. Kernel-based windowing codes and operating systems share the same physical memory space and are accessed in essentially the same way.

Client-Server Architecture

Client-server architectures provide a means for sharing windowing-system resources among multiple processes and machines. A server is a computer running software that provides a particular capability to an entire network of interconnected machines. A client is a piece of software on the same network that requests and uses the capabilities provided by the server.

Even the best client-server implementations incur significant communication overhead that can lead to noticeable performance degradation compared to kernel-based windowing systems. Kernel-based systems achieve higher performance at the cost of device dependence and the need to redundantly execute the same code on each machine.

Window Management

Window-management facilities allow the system to maintain spatial relationships between windows as they are moved, resized, and depth-arranged. Several options are available in window control menus that feature automatic arrangement of windows. Of particular importance are tiled, overlapping, and cascading windows. While the historical controversy over the relative merits of tiled and overlapping windows appears to have been resolved in favor of overlapping window management, tiled windows may still be useful in large or high-resolution displays.

Tiled Windows

Tiled windows are arranged automatically by the windowing system to completely fill the available display space (which may be either the entire display screen or an entire content area of a window). Windows are prevented from overlapping. When any window is resized, other windows must be sized in the opposing direction to compensate.

Overlapping Windows

Overlapping windows have an associated depth value that represents their distance from the viewer. At each pixel, only the contents of the nearest window covering that portion of the display are presented. The window with the lowest depth value thus obscures the contents of any other windows occupying the same display space, creating an illusion of physical overlapping. The resulting window stack is comparable to a pile of papers on the user's desk and allows users to take advantage of existing spatial-management skills.

Cascading Windows

Cascading windows are a special case of overlapping window management in which the windows are arranged automatically in a regular progression that prevents any window from being completely obscured. The origins (that is the upper-left corner) of each successive window is offset slightly in both the horizontal and vertical directions to conserve display space while simplifying the task of bringing any window to the front of the stack.

Imaging Model

The imaging model is embodied in the set of functions used by the window manager to translate mathematical

descriptions of graphical elements into pixel images in
the physical buffers of the display device. The two major
classes of imaging model are based on raster images
(bitmaps) that correspond directly to the resolution of
the output device or on vector-based drawing languages
such as PostScript, which maps abstract procedural
image descriptions to the physical coordinates of the
output device.

Because the image is defined procedurally and must be
decoded by the windowing-system software, the rendering time for a vector-based language such as Display
PostScript is dependent on the complexity of the image
involved. Raster-based models, in contrast, provide rendering speed that is independent of image complexity.

The coordinate system, color capabilities, and image
transfer mode defined by the imaging model can significantly affect the performance of the windowing system
and the quality of the displays it can support. Device-
dependent imaging models produce optimum performance, but may constrain the quality of printed output
and produce displays that must be recoded whenever the
platform changes. Sophisticated, device-independent imaging models can be scaled to match the resolution of
any output devices, but the transformations may notice-
ably reduce rendering speed.

X Window System   The X Window System, developed jointly by MIT and
DEC, is becoming rapidly the de facto standard for GUIs
in workstation- and network-computing environments.
X, V. 11 (X11) provides a high-throughput, network-
transparent mechanism permitting communication between client programs and window servers.

Either the client, the server, or both may reside on the
local machine. The X Window System provides a sub-
strate for network communications and imaging across
a wide variety of displays that is totally independent of
the appearance and behavior of the GUI layer. Both Motif and OPEN LOOK leverage this capability by providing variations in appearance and behavior on top of the
basic X11 functionality.

Windowing-System Components

The appearance and behavior of the windowing system as experienced by the user is determined by a small group of standard components. The systems make use of essentially the same set of human-interface objects, but the names by which these components are identified vary significantly among vendors (see Fig. A.1, Appendix A). The following set of terms will streamline cross-product comparisons by identifying standard components consistently and unambiguously.

Windows

From the viewpoint of the window manager, a window is any discrete area of the visual display that can be moved, sized, and rendered independently on the display screen. Even though most of the components are actually implemented and managed as windows by the system, we consider windows from the user's point of view. The definition we employ will therefore include only those display objects that allow the user to change the view of their contents using techniques such as sizing, scrolling, or editing.

Menus

Menus provide users with a means of command retrieval that enables them to see and point instead of remembering and typing. The menu system allows problems caused by the limitations of human memory to be greatly reduced at the expense of slightly reduced motor performance. The benefits are substantial, particularly when the number and complexity of commonly used applications limits the user's expertise with individual command sets.

Controls

Any visually represented window component that can be manipulated directly with the mouse or keyboard is a control. Each of the windowing systems defines standard sets of controls that can be incorporated by applications to provide consistent interaction protocols across products.

Dialogue Boxes

Dialogue boxes provide a visual and functional context for presenting options from which the user can select. Any interactive exchange of information between the user and the system that takes place in a limited spatial context considered a dialogue.

Although three distinct classes of dialogue box are described (control panels, query boxes, and message boxes), there may be considerable overlap between classes. Any dialogue box can be characterized by a clearly defined scope that determines the effect on the state of the system and the subsequent operations permitted.

Modeless Dialogues

Modeless dialogue boxes are limited in scope and do not restrict the subsequent operations of the user. Modeless dialogues may incorporate some basic window functions such as sizing and positioning. Users can continue to work without responding, if necessary, and may be allowed to keep the modeless dialogue on display even after a response has been made.

Modal Dialogues

Modal dialogue boxes require the user to respond before any other action can be taken. Application modal dialogues prevent the user from invoking any application functions until the dialogue has been satisfied, while system modal dialogues prevent the user from performing any operations anywhere in the system.

Control Panels

Control panels appear at the implicit or explicit request of the user and provide information reflecting the current state of a number of related system parameters, any of which can be changed interactively while the panel remains on display. Changes to the system state do not take effect until the user explicitly accepts the new settings.

Query Boxes

Query boxes appear in response to user actions, but are not requested explicitly by the user. Query boxes prompt the user for a single piece of information, such as a yes-or-no answer to a single question, and provide a context in which the necessary information can be provided. Like control panels, query boxes allow the user to cancel the action that led to the query.

Message Boxes

Providing critical information to the user is the primary function of message boxes, which are not requested by the user and typically appear only when the system has entered, or is about to enter, an unrecoverable and potentially dangerous state. The user's response options are typically limited to a simple yes-or-no decision, or in irreversible system states, simple acknowledgment of the message.

Mouse/Keyboard Interface

The systems use a mouse and keyboard as the primary interaction devices. Each device is well-suited to certain types of interaction tasks. The mouse provides an efficient means of accomplishing tasks that require spatial manipulation, such as menu navigation and window sizing and positioning. The keyboard is more efficient for sequential tasks, such as text entry and window shuffling.

Conclusion

Having discussed briefly the differences of implementation, I shall discuss the various typical components of window systems in the following sections.

7.3 Windows

Introduction

The windowing systems discussed in this chapter all provide a standard window structure within which application programs and documents are displayed for and controlled by the user. Most of these systems define a number of standard window types that can be

customized by applications as necessary. For the purpose of comparison, this section describes standard
windows that implement the basic features provided by
the windowing system.

Application and
Document Windows

An application window is the first object that appears
in the workspace when a program is launched. The application window may contain data itself or it may provide a top-level context for one or more "child"
windows (that is, dependent windows created by the independent, or "parent," window) that actually contain
the data being processed. Child windows containing
data that can be freely modified by the user are usually
described as document windows, because they are typically associated with a single data object such as a text
file or drawing.

The structure of document windows is similar or
identical to that of application windows. Document
windows provide a context within which to store and
display the data for a single object as it is being created. Most applications support multiple document windows that allow users to work with more than one file
at a time. The parent window's application menu af-
fects only the document window that is currently receiving user input.

Window Icons

Window icons conserve display space by reducing the
size of windows during periods in which no input from
the user is required. Window icons help the user to
maintain a global context by providing a visual reminder of the currently active applications and documents.
These icons also allow previous local contexts to be
immediately restored through direct interaction with
visible objects.

Overall Appearance

A recent trend in GUIs is the creation of windows and
window components that appear to be three-
dimensional, resembling real-world controls on familiar devices such as automotive dashboards or hi-fi
equipment. The stylistic treatment has useful functional
implications as well, because raised three-dimensional

Macintosh

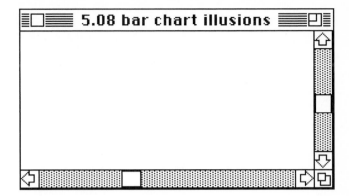

NextStep

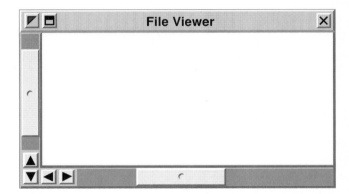

OPEN LOOK

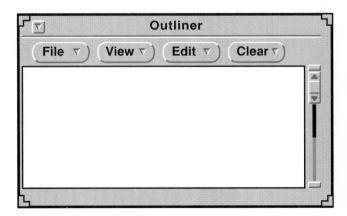

Figure 7.1 Window Systems Gallery 1

OSF/Motif

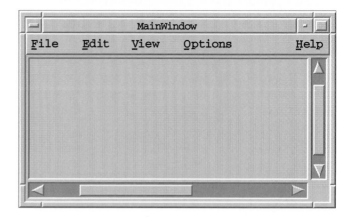

Microsoft Windows 3.0

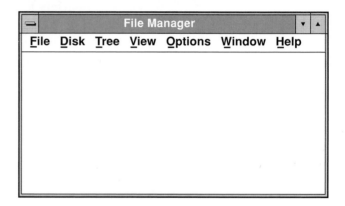

OS/2 Presentation Manager

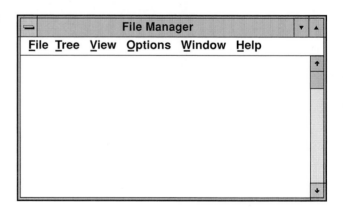

Figure 7.2 Window Systems Gallery 2

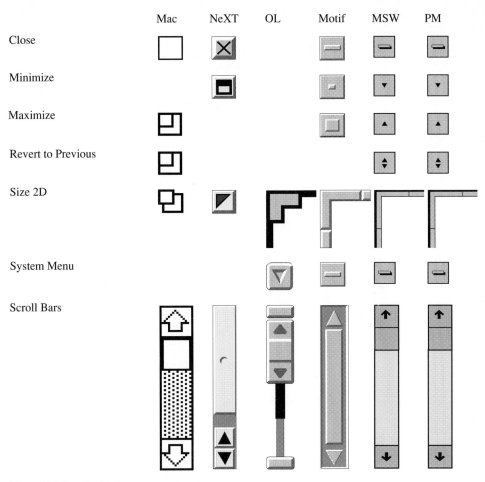

Figure 7.3 Standard Window Controls

areas can be easily differentiated from their surroundings and identified as graspable or pushable objects.

Window Structure

The structure of application and document windows varies considerably across systems. Most windows have a border region controlled by the windowing system and a content region that the application can freely modify. The Windowing System Galleries pictured in Figs. 7.1 and 7.2 provide a visual catalogue of the overall structure and major components of a full-featured basic window in each of the six systems. See Figs. B.1 and B.2 for an annotated version identifying components using system-specific terminology.

**Standard
Window Controls**

As the technology of windowing systems has matured, the set of standard user controls for window management and manipulation has become relatively stable (see Fig. 7.3). The system-specific details of each of these fundamental window-management operations are described more extensively in Section 7.8.

Conclusion

Windows provide the means of displaying application-related data. To modify the data, menus are required to provide the relevant functions. The various kinds of menus are discussed in the following section.

7.4 Menus

Introduction

Menus provide a means for the user to issue commands without having to remember the name and syntax of the particular command required. Each of the window systems being compared uses the select-then-operate command paradigm. The user first selects the object or objects to which the operation is to apply, then chooses the appropriate command from the menu.

The six windowing systems each provide a menu interface for the majority of their capabilities. At the most general level, the systems all display menus as vertical lists of commands. Beyond this, however, the appearance and behavior of menus varies substantially across systems. Figures 7.4 and 7.5 display a representative sample of the standard menus provided by each system. The following discussion describes the major differences in menu appearance, behavior, and standardization across applications. This section will define a limited number of menu classes based on these fundamental menu characteristics. Some further distinctions bear mentioning: representation, duration, and navigation.

Representation: Implicit pop-up menus appear whenever the mouse menu button is depressed within a particular region of the display. The region may be the entire screen or some well-defined area such as a window or window border, but no feedback is provided to remind the user of the presence of a menu. In explicit pop-up menus, areas from which menus can be accessed are designated by a specific symbol or visual treatment applied to a standard control. A special case is the pull-down menu, in which the menu is attached to a menu bar at the top of the window or the display screen.

Duration: The presentation of a menu may be either static, with the menu displayed continuously in a particular location, or dynamic, with the menu displayed only until the user makes a selection. Stay-up menus provide a combination of these behaviors. These menus are positioned in a convenient location and remain on display even after a selection has been made, allowing the user to select repeatedly from the options presented.

Navigation: Menu hierarchies are traversed by using the mouse menu button with either apress-drag-release or a click-position-click protocol. Except for the Macintosh, each of the six windowing systems supports both methods of selection.

Menu Appearance

The visible language characteristics of the menu can strengthen the conceptual model of the GUI presented by the windowing system. The visible language used to reflect the state of the menu items must represent (1) the currently selected state of any multistate item or group of items, (2) the eligibility of an item for selection, (3) the presence of attached submenus or dialogue boxes, and (4) the keyboard shortcut that can be used to access a particular item. Appropriate visual feedback must also be provided to identify the menu item currently selected by the mouse pointer or key-board cursor as the user navigates through the menu system.

In each of the windowing systems, items that cannot be selected are emphasized less than valid selections. Attached submenus are represented by arrows or triangles, while dialogue boxes are represented by the ellipsis character (see Fig. 7.4). OPEN LOOK is the only system that does not provide explicit representation of keyboard menu shortcuts. The other systems all place the name of the "accelerator," or "hot," key and its qualifiers at the right edge of the associated menu item.

Macintosh

NeXT

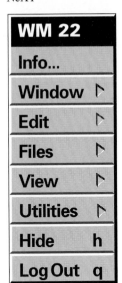

OPEN LOOK

Motif

MS Windows

Presentation Manager

File	
Open	Enter
Print...	
Move...	F7
Delete...	Del
Select All	Ctrl+/
Exit	

File	
Open	Enter
Print...	ShiftPrtSet
Move...	F7
Delete...	Delete
Select All	Ctrl+/
Exit	F3

Figure 7.4 Menu Gallery

	Mac	NeXT	OL	Motif	MSW	PM
Pull-Down Menus	●		●	●	●	●
Implicit Pop-Up Menus		●	●	●	●	●
Explicit Pop-Up Menus	●	●	●			
Stay-up Menus	●	●	●			

Figure 7.5 Menu
Presentation Techniques

Menu Behavior

The behavioral aspects of menus constrain the ways in which they can be manipulated by the user and the manner in which they respond to user interaction. Individual classes of menus can be described by their representation, duration, and navigation characteristics. Except for NextStep, the systems all support pulldown menus attached to the individual application or document windows or (on the Macintosh) to the top of the display screen. Each system also provides pop-up menus represented either implicitly or explicitly (see Fig. 7.5).

Standard Menus and Menu Items

The standard menus items defined by each windowing system are listed in Fig. 7.6 Menus containing windowing-system commands are generally provided by the system itself. Other menus are defined by the application and may differ from the system menus in presentation or behavior. Both types of menu rely on standardization to help users locate the desired command.

Window-Control Menus

Task- and window-management functions allow multiple windows to share display space. The Macintosh and NextStep provide only a few of these system-level functions in the same set of menus used by application programs. Users of these systems must rely on the controls provided in the window borders for most of their window-management tasks. The remaining systems place window-control functions in menus that are physically or conceptually distinguished from the menus used by application programs.

Mac	NeXT	OL	Motif	MSW	PM
	Info	File	System	Control	System
File	Window	View		File	File
Edit	Edit	Edit		Edit	Edit
		Props		View	View
				Window	Window
				Help	Help

Figure 7.6 Standard
Menu Commands

Component Menus

OPEN LOOK provides implicit pop-up menus for various structural regions of the window as well as for certain controls such as textfields, scrollbars, and scrolling lists. These component menus, which are required for conforming to OPEN LOOK implementations, are described in greater detail in Appendix B.

Application Menus

Applications normally require their own set of menus, which may be presented separately or integrated with the system menus in both application and document windows. Some application functions are universal and appear in the menus of virtually every program. If the names and locations in the menu structure of these common functions vary significantly across applications, the system may be unnecessarily difficult to learn and use. Most windowing systems therefore provide recommendations or standards to produce a menu configuration that is consistent across applications (see Fig. 7.7).

Conclusion

Additional adjustments of application windows that cannot be accomplished with the menus directly require further adjustment of data. The data parameters and their annotation are provided by controls, which are discussed in the following section.

7.5 Controls and Control Panels

Introduction

Effectively designed controls allow the GUI to produce a convincing illusion of interaction with concrete physical objects. Because they are similar in both appearance and behavior to buttons, knobs, and switches, controls

	Mac	NeXT*	OL	Motif	MSW	PM
Move				●	●	●
Size		●		●	●	●
Minimize		●	●	●	●	●
Maximize			●	●	●	●
Restore			●	●	●	●
End Application		●	●		●	●
Place Front Window Behind Others			●	●		
Refresh Display			●			
Change Window Properties			●			

Figure 7.7 Window Control Menu Commands

permit users to exploit knowledge they already possess. This section reviews the standard controls provided by each of the systems and the standard dialogue contexts in which they are presented to the user. An example of the standard context in which this dialogue takes place is seen in the representative control panel in Fig. 7.8. Although the behavior of a given type of control is generally consistent across systems, its visual representation may vary substantially (see Fig. 7.9 and 7.10).

Standard Controls

Each of the six windowing systems defines a limited set of standard control types that form the basis for the control panels created by the application developer. The set of standard controls available across systems provide a way to see and modify five essential classes of information: exclusive settings; nonexclusive settings; proportional-slider controls; text fields and lists; and command buttons.

Exclusive Settings

Exclusive settings provide a way to select exactly one value from a group of possibilities. The preset buttons commonly seen on car radios provide a familiar metaphor that is frequently used to represent the concept to the user.

Nonexclusive Settings

Nonexclusive settings are lists of attributes or properties that can be independently set and cleared by the user. Any number of nonexclusive settings can be indicated simultaneously.

Proportional-Slider Controls

Proportional sliders are used to represent any variable that can be modified continuously within a well-defined range. Sliders are well-suited to display any parameter with more options than can be represented comfortably using exclusive settings. Dials and gauges provide the same type of information in a passive form that cannot be modified by the user.

Text Fields and Lists

Text fields allow the user to place alphanumeric data into the system and support a limited set of editing functions. Lists may provide editing capabilities as well, but typically they are read-only devices used primarily for selection from groups of existing objects. Scrolling lists are used for groups with too many items to be displayed in the space allocated to the list. The standard window scrollbars or more general proportional slider controls are used to determine the displayed portion of the list.

Command Buttons

Command buttons represent instructions to perform a particular system action. Unlike the other standard controls, they produce an immediate change in the state of the system. Command buttons provide the equivalent of a menu command in an immediately available format that allows the user to avoid navigation through the menu system.

Command buttons are distinguished from other controls by their ability to produce an immediate system response. Pressing or clicking a "cancel" button in a control panel, for example, returns the system to its former state and causes the panel to disappear. Like menu items, command buttons may convey information such as their eligibility for selection or existence of an attached menu or a dialogue box. The visual treatments applied to command buttons by the various windowing

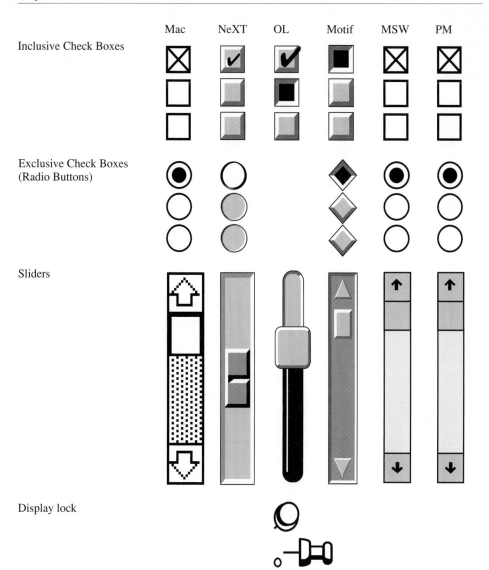

Inclusive Check Boxes

Exclusive Check Boxes
(Radio Buttons)

Sliders

Display lock

Figure 7.8 Standard Control Presentations

Mac   NeXT   OL   Motif   MSW/PM

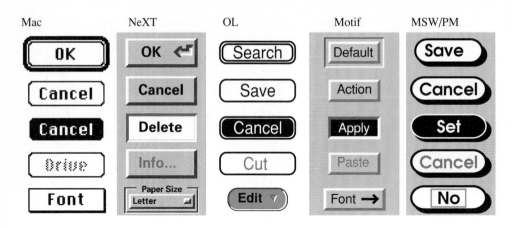

Figure 7.9 Standard   systems to represent these and other button states are
Button Vocabularies   shown in Fig. 7.9.

Control Panels   Control panels, and dialogue boxes in general, usually
                           provide the user with a preselected default response
                           that can be accepted with a simple action such as
                           pressing the keyboard return key. The default response
                           is normally assigned to the command button selected
                           most frequently, except in situations where the most
                           common command leads to an operation that is irre-
                           versible or potentially dangerous. The default button is
                           identified by adding visual information (such as a
                           thickened border) that increases its perceptual promi-
                           nence (see Figs. 7.9 and 7.10).

                           Standard control panels for frequently needed func-
                           tions are defined by each of the windowing systems
                           (see Fig. 7.11). The standard panel designs increase the
                           consistency of user interaction across applications.
                           Even though the individual applications may need to
                           modify the default control panels, the presence of a
                           consistent basic structure can provide some degree of
                           familiarity for fundamental tasks even in programs that
                           differ greatly from one another. The process of learn-
                           ing new applications as well as the system itself is sim-
                           plified when the standard designs achieve widespread
                           acceptance.

Conclusion   Although controls and control panels provide a direct
                           means for the user interacting with the computer, other

Figure 7.10 Representative
Control Panel (NextStep)

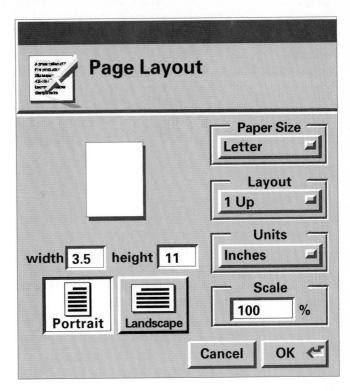

exchanges of command control and status reporting are
often required. The various query and message boxes
provide the means of sustaining this dialogue. They are
discussed in the following section.

7.6 Query and Message Boxes

Introduction

Query and message boxes (see Figs. 7.12 and 7.13) are
initiated by the application, not the user. Like control
panels, these boxes are special cases of the more general class of dialogue boxes. Query boxes are normally
modal as well, but the user may be permitted to reposi-
tion the box during some queries in order to examine
other information contained in the display. Message
boxes always initiate a modal context in which one of
the available options must be explicitly selected by the
user before any further operations can take place.

Query Boxes

Query boxes allow the system to request a specific
piece of information from the user. They typically
prompt the user for the necessary information in the

	Mac	NeXT	OL	Motif	MSW	PM
Open File	●	●		●	●	●
Save File As...	●	●		●	●	●
Page Setup	●	●				
Choose Printer	●	●			●	●
Print File	●	●			●	●
Choose Font		●				
User Preferences	●	●	●		●	●

Figure 7.11 Standard Control Panels

form of a question; such as, "Are you sure you want to delete the file: Final Section?"

Message Boxes

Message boxes provide notification that a dangerous or illegal state has been entered. Often there is no chance for recovery and the user is merely alerted so that collateral damage can be minimized. The user may be presented with several response options, but more frequently the user is allowed only to acknowledge the receipt of the message before the system attempts to deal with the problem. In each of the windowing systems, the appearance of a message box is accompanied by an audible beep to attract the user's attention.

Conclusion

Dialogue boxes often embody significant cognitive tasks, that is, the user's view of the work being done. Their correct design is often a key factor of good product design.

7.7 Mouse/Keyboard Interface

Introduction

This section describes essential characteristics of the mouse interaction of graphical interfaces.

Mouse-Button Functions

The same set of basic commands is used in each of the windowing systems. There are three basic functions (select, menu, and adjust), which are supported in every windowing system. When less than three mouse buttons are available, keyboard qualifiers or the location of the pointer must be used to determine the operation being indicated by the user.

Select: The select function is used to manipulate controls and data objects within the display and to select

Figure 7.12 Representative
Query Box

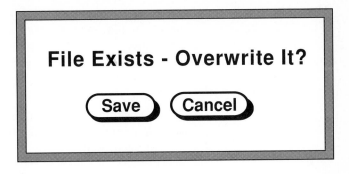

Figure 7.13 Representative
Message Box

objects that will be affected by subsequent operations
(that is, menu commands). The select function is the
most important of the three and is universally assigned
to the first available mouse button.

Menu: The menu function is typically used to display
an implicit pop-up menu. The availability of a dedicated
menu button allows the pop-up menu to be associated
with any portion of the display, as the menu function is
invoked by the identity of the button producing the
event, not the location of the pointer.

Adjust: The adjust function extends or reduces the number of selected items. It is needed less frequently than
either the menu or select functions and is there-fore the
last to be implemented on a dedicated mouse button.

Mouse-Button Actions   A limited set of actions can be performed with any mouse button. Five operations (point, click, double-click, press, and drag) form the primitive vocabulary on which mouse-based interaction with the system is based.

Point: Position the mouse pointer so that the pixel-level selection point (the "hot spot") rests within the desired area of the display screen.

Click: Point to the item of interest, then depress and immediately release a mouse button without moving the mouse.

Double-Click: Point to the item of interest, then depress and release the mouse button twice in rapid succession without moving the mouse.

Press: Point to the item of interest, then depress the mouse button and hold it down.

Drag: Press the mouse button on the item of interest. While keeping the button depressed, move the mouse in the appropriate direction.

Combination Mouse and Keyboard Operations   Users who make infrequent use of the mouse in keyboard-intensive applications may be severely inconvenienced by operations that require a combination of mouse and keyboard input. The relatively high cost of removing a hand from the keyboard, finding and operating the mouse, and returning the hand to the proper keyboard location may offset any positioning advantage offered by the mouse.

In situations with limited keyboard data-entry requirements, however, a small number of keyboard qualifiers can extend the available set of mouse functions in a logically consistent and easily understandable manner. In some situations, combination keyboard and mouse operations cannot be avoided. OPEN LOOK implementations using a one-button mouse, for example, must forfeit the power and flexibility provided by the various implicit pop-up menus unless a keyboard menu qualifier is available.

Although the mouse provides the primary means of manipulating windows and controls, each windowing system provides some level of access to the functionality of the windowing system from the keyboard as well. For Motif, Windows, and Presentation Manager, the explicit goal is to provide a keyboard equivalent for every system function.

Mouse-Pointer Image   Context-dependent changes to the image of the mouse pointer can provide the user with meaningful visual feedback on the current state of the system. Because the pointer is normally the focus of the user's attention, it can immediately alert the user when an unintended action has been performed. The pointer image also helps users remain oriented by providing a constant reminder of the current mode of operation. Standard pointer images for the various systems are shown in Fig.7.14.

Pointer Jumping   An unusual characteristic of OPEN LOOK is the automatic movement of the mouse pointer during situations in which the system "knows" where the user would like the pointer to be placed. This behavior called Pointer Jumping, is described more completely in Section 7.8 and Appendix B.

Mouse-Button Mappings   Except for the Macintosh and NextStep, the windowing systems can each be used with a one-, two-, or three-button mouse. When more than one button is available, users must remember which button to click or press to produce the desired result. The problem is simplified by substantial agreement on the logical categories (select, menu, etc.) that mouse functions are placed in (see Fig. 7.15).

Keyboard Focus   The active window is described as having the keyboard focus because it receives any characters type by the user until another window is made active. Windows must usually acquire the keyboard focus before they can be manipulated by the user, even in operations that

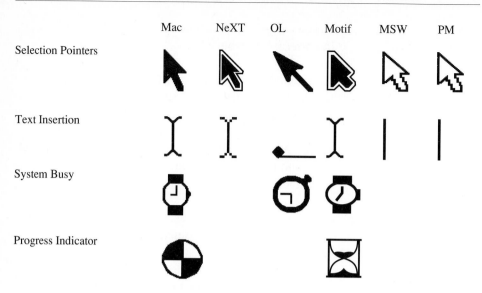

	Mac	NeXT	OL	Motif	MSW	PM

Selection Pointers

Text Insertion

System Busy

Progress Indicator

Figure 7.14 Standard
Mouse Pointer Images

do not require the use of the keyboard. OPEN LOOK provides an exception to this policy by permitting windows to be selected and manipulated without receiving the keyboard focus.

Most windowing systems identify the active window by altering the appearance of the window's title bar. Motif can provide global color coding as well by changing the colors of the entire display to match a palette provided by the window with the keyboard focus.

Keyboard Window Management

Keyboard-driven window-management commands eliminate the effort required to move and position the mouse in large, high-resolution displays. Keyboard window management also provides access to operations that frequently cannot be performed directly with the mouse.

Keyboard control is particularly valuable in situations where overlapping window management permits smaller windows to be completely obscured by larger windows. Instead of dragging the obscuring windows out of the way, the keyboard user can cycle through the windows, bringing them one after another to the front of the window stack until the desired window is located.

	Mac	NeXT	OL	Motif	MSW	PM
One-button	select	n/a	select	select	select	select
Two-button (left)	n/a	select	select	select	select	select
Two-button (right)	n/a	adjust*	menu	menu	cancel	cancel
Three-button (left)	n/a	n/a	select	select	select	select
Three-button (middle)	n/a	n/a	adjust	menu	cancel	cancel
Three-button (right)	n/a	n/a	menu	free	free	free

Figure 7.15 Default
Mouse Button Mappings

Because of their bias in favor of the mouse and their goal of presenting a simple and consistent conceptual model, the Macintosh and NextStep limit keyboard access to system-level functions. The four remaining systems offer a much wider range of options, as detailed in Section 7.8.

Keyboard Menu Shortcuts

Each of the windowing systems provides keyboard shortcuts for commonly used menu commands. This capability is important for touch typists, particularly in applications where use of the mouse is secondary due to the human-performance costs associated with removing a hand from the keyboard. The keyboard shortcut, or accelerator, is represented explicitly in the menu item in each of the systems except OPEN LOOK, in which keyboard shortcuts are not supported.

Keyboard Menu Navigation

Motif, Windows, and Presentation Manager provide an alternative method for accessing menu and control-panel items entirely through the keyboard. Instead of the single key combination provided by menu accelerators, keyboard navigation allows users to browse through the menu system with arrow keys and the space bar. Query boxes and control panels are navigated using the space-bar, tab, and enter keys. Appendix B provides a more complete description of the process.

Keyboard Pointer Control

OPEN LOOK supports mouseless hardware configurations by permitting the keyboard to emulate mouse operations. The arrow keys are used to move the pointer, whose appearance and behavior are the same as when the mouse is present. Any mouse-button function can be mapped to any keystroke combination through user-preferences dialogue boxes, which allow the user to define conventions for any required behavior.

Conclusion

The preceding sections have reviewed individual basic characteristics of the window systems. The next section considers how these systems enable typical window-management tasks to be accomplished.

7.8 Analysis of Common Tasks

Introduction

The following discussion reviews the steps required to accomplish a number of frequently encountered tasks in each of the six windowing systems. The selected tasks are both diagnostic and representative of the operations performed routinely by the user.

Move Windows

The six windowing systems all permit the user to move windows by using the select button to drag within the title bar. OPEN LOOK permits dragging by either side border as well as by the header at the top of the window. This capability may substantially reduce the amount of mouse movement required in a high-resolution display. Motif, Windows, and Presentation Manager also allow the user to move windows using only the keyboard.

Size Windows

The windowing systems differ substantially in operation and presentation of the sizing controls and in the visual feedback provided during the resizing process (see Fig. 7.16).

The Macintosh provides a single sizing control in the lower-right corner of the window. To enlarge a window toward the top or left side of the screen, the user must first drag the window in the direction of the size increase, then drag the right and bottom borders into the desired position using the sizing control. NextStep provides slightly more flexibility by allowing users to resize the window from the lower border or from either of the lower corners.

OPEN LOOK windows allow sizing mechanisms in all four corners, as well as a unique capability that provides uniform scaling of windows and their contents. After manipulating a slider control to enlarge or reduce the window, the user views the results by pressing a button to apply the new parameters. The scaling capability can be used to conserve display space, to prioritize document windows, or to ease the editing of documents containing text in very small point sizes.

Motif, Windows, and Presentation Manager provide the most flexible set of resizing controls, with handles in each corner and on each side. This scheme has the advantage of being easily understood as there is a consistently applied logic in the placement of handles along the axis of movement for any resizing operation that might be desired. By invoking the resize option from the window control menu, the keyboard and arrow keys can also be used to adjust the window borders.

Motif, Windows, and Presentation Manager are also the only systems that change the pointer image when a sizing control is successfully selected with the mouse. Pausing with the pointer over any of the sizing controls changes the image from the default-selection arrow into a two- or four-headed arrow reflecting the path along which the border may freely be moved. The visual feedback provided by the changing pointer image reminds the user of the border's function and increases the ease of selecting the relatively narrow controls.

Change Window Focus

Because only one window can be attached to the keyboard at a time, users must be able to identify and reassign the window receiving the stream of characters. The simple conceptual model presented by Macintosh and NextStep permits windows to receive the focus only after they have been brought to the front of the display. To type in a window, the user simply clicks anywhere within its borders.

Windows in OPEN LOOK receive the keyboard focus (called Input Area) automatically when the mouse select or adjust button is clicked within any area in which text can be inserted. An optional configuration causes the focus to change whenever the mouse pointer enters a window. The focus can also be changed from the keyboard. The user can cycle the focus through the window stack

	Mac	NeXT	OL	Motif	MSW	PM
Size Window from Keyboard				●	●	●
Size Window from Left Side (1D)				●	●	●
Size Window from Right Side (1D)				●	●	●
Size Window from Top (1D)				●	●	●
Size Window from Bottom (1D)	●			●	●	●
Size Window from Upper LH Corner			●	●	●	●
Size Window from Upper RH Corner			●	●	●	●
Size Window from Lower LH Corner		●	●	●	●	●
Size Window from Lower RH Corner	●	●	●	●	●	●

Figure 7.16 Window
Sizing Capabilities

without altering the depth arrangement of individual windows. The order of cycling proceeds from most to the least recently used window or vice versa. The keyboard can also be used to toggle the focus between the two most recently used windows.

Motif can also be configured to automatically focus on a window when the user moves the pointer in front of the window. The default behavior, however, changes the keyboard focus only when the user clicks within the window boundaries. The keyboard focus can also be cycled through the window stack in either direction using the alternate, shift, and tab keys. By default, Motif does not automatically raise windows to the front of the stack as they receive the keyboard focus, but the system can be configured to do so. Motif is unique in allowing the keyboard focus to be cycled through a user or application-defined subset of the windows and icons on display.

In Windows and Presentation Manager, windows can receive the keyboard focus only at the front of the stack. A number of keyboard operations that simultaneously alter the depth arrangement and focus of the windows are described in the following subsection.

Change Window Depth

Depth arrangement of overlapping windows is a task that is performed more frequently than either moving or sizing. The efficiency of the mechanism provided to accomplish this task is therefore a critical determinant of the usability of the resulting system. Each of the systems allows the user to bring a partially covered window to the front of the display by clicking anywhere inside its borders with the mouse select button (see Fig. 7.17).In the Macintosh human interface, this is the only depth-arrangement mechanism provided. The remaining systems provide numerous variations on this fundamental depth-arrangement technique.

NextStep allows windows to be brought to the front of the display without giving them the keyboard focus, but requires the user to qualify the mouse click with the alternate key. This inspection capability is particularly important in systems based on the client-server architecture, because changing the active window will require communication between at least two applications. The technique permits the delay imposed by network communication overhead to be avoided in situations where the user wants only to check the contents of the inactive window.

OPEN LOOK windows can also be brought forward without receiving the keyboard focus by clicking the mouse select button anywhere within their borders *except* within a text field. An option in the OPEN LOOK window control menu can be used to push the window to the back of the display. This technique is useful when a large window at the front of the stack impedes access to windows in the rear.

Like OPEN LOOK, Motif provides a window-to-back (called Lower) option in the window control menu that moves the front window to the back of the stack and replaces it with the second window. Keyboard commands extend this capability by permitting the user to shuffle the windows from front to back or back to front without altering their focus. The logical keystroke events that invoke these functions may be assigned by the user to any of the available physical keys.

Users of Windows and Presentation Manager can cycle the stack in either direction, swap the two front windows, or preview the windows from front to back before activating one of them and bringing it automatically to

	Mac	NeXT	OL	Motif	MSW	PM
Bring Window to Front and Auto-Focus	●	●		●	●	●
Bring Window to Front Without Focusing		●	●			
Focus Window without Altering Depth			●	●		
Move Window without Altering Depth	●		●	●		
Size Window without Altering Depth			●	●		
Cycle Window Focus but not Depth			●	●		
Cycle Window Depth but not Focus			●	●		
Cycle Window Focus and Depth					●	●

Figure 7.17 Window Focus and Depth Arrangement

the front without changing the relative depths of the remaining windows. In the preview mode, windows and icons are opened to their full size, but only the border and title bar of each window are displayed. Because the window contents are not drawn, the process can be repeated at high speed until the user finds the desired window. These operations are accomplished from the keyboard using combinations of the alternate, escape, shift, and spacebar keys.

Scroll Window Contents

Scrolling through documents or spaces larger than the physical size of the window through which they are viewed is a task encountered frequently in every windowing system. The design of the scrolling mechanism and the types of behavior it supports can significantly affect performance in this critical task.

Scroll Bars

Scroll bars are needed whenever the size of the data being presented is greater than that of the space available for displaying it. The typical scroll bar contains three basic elements: scroll container, scroll handle, and scroll arrows (see Fig. 7.18).

Scroll Container

The scroll container is the track within which the scroll handle moves. The motion of the scroll handle is normally limited to the horizontal or vertical axis, but two-dimensional scrolling controls that can be adjusted in both directions simultaneously are possible.

Scroll Handle

The scroll handle is the object identifying the current
location within the data file being displayed. By dragging the scroll handle with the mouse pointer, the user
can change the portion of the document appearing in
the window.

Scroll Arrows

Two scroll arrows are present in each scroll bar to provide line-by-line scrolling toward the outer limits of the
data object. In the moving-window paradigm, scroll arrows indicate the direction in which the window frame
moves when the arrow is clicked or pressed. The data
region appears to move in the opposite directions.

Scroll Comparison

In the six windowing systems, the scrollbar is manipulated with the mouse select button. Scrollbars, by definition, allow the user to select the scroll handle and
drag it with the mouse to any position within the scroll
container. The behavior of scroll arrows is also consistent across systems. Clicking the scroll arrow moves
the window contents by a single line. When the arrow
is pressed, the contents of the window are scrolled continuously until the mouse button is released.

Each of the systems uses the scrolling model based on
a moving window, rather than moving data. In the
moving-window model, pressing a scroll arrow or
dragging the scroll handle causes the contents of the
window to scroll smoothly in the direction opposite the
one indicated by the arrow or the direction of movement of the scroll handle. While the mapping may
seem unnatural, testing has demonstrated a clear preference for this model among users.

The scrolling behavior (see Fig. 7.19) incorporated by
the Macintosh human interface is the simplest of any of
the six windowing systems. Macintosh users can page
through the document (scroll by window-sized incre-
ments) by pressing or repeatedly clicking the mouse

button anywhere within the scroll container, but this capability is the only enhancement of the basic scrolling technique.

Scroll arrows on the Macintosh are placed at opposite ends of the scroll container. This placement maximizes the clarity of the conceptual model because the mouse is moved in the same direction (that is, away from the current position) when either the scroll arrow or the scroll handle is manipulated. In all but the smallest windows, however, the large separation of the scroll arrows can significantly increase the effort required to adjust the window contents by scrolling in alternating directions.

The direction switching problem is resolved in Next-Step by positioning the scroll arrows side by side at one end of the container. This placement simplifies repeated forward and backward scrolling, but eliminates the spatial correspondence between the beginning, the middle, and the end of the document.

NextStep users can move directly to any position in the document by clicking in the region of the scroll container corresponding to the desired position. The scroll handle moves immediately to the point indicated by the cursor and the window contents are modified to reflect the new position. The relatively complex process of placing the mouse pointer on the scroll handle, pressing the mouse select button, and holding it down while dragging the scroll handle into the desired location is replaced by a simple point and click.

NextStep also allows the user to page through the document by pressing the alternate key while clicking inside the scroll container. The scroll handle itself is used to represent the proportion of the document that is currently visible within the window. As the document grows, the scroll handle is reduced in length. Of the six systems, only the NextStep scrollbar does not provide visual feedback (highlighting, reverse video, etc.) when the scroll handle has been selected with the pointer.

Figure 7.18 Standard
Window Scrollbars

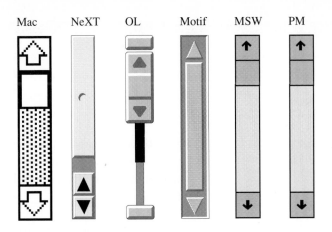

Scrollbars in OPEN LOOK are based on a relatively
complex conceptual model incorporating extended functionality and multiple modes of operation. OPEN LOOK
scrollbars, for example, are always associated with an
implicit pop-up menu that allows the user to move to the
beginning or end of the document or to move directly to
the previous location within the document. The required
scrollbar menu also allows the user to split the window
or join previously split segments.

OPEN LOOK scrollbars can be manipulated from the
keyboard also, which provides logical keybindings for
scrolling by line or page and for moving directly to
either end or side of a document. The user can move
directly to the beginning or end of the document by
clicking on one of the perpendicular bars at either end
of the scroll container. Unlike NextStep, however, the
click-to-position behavior does not extend to the interior
of the scroll container itself. Clicking within this region
pages the window contents and moves the scroll handle
toward the pointer.

Unlike the other systems, OPEN LOOK dims a scroll
arrow when movement in the corresponding direction is
not possible. When the entire document appears within
a window, both arrows are dimmed. When only a portion of the document is visible, the black line representing the axis of movement in the scrollbar is partially
thickened to provide an indicator of what proportion of

	Mac	NeXT	OL	Motif	MSW	PM
Drag to position	●	●	●	●	●	●
Scroll smoothly (by line)	●	●	●	●	●	●
Scroll by window-sized pages	●	●*	●	●	●	●
Click to beginning/end of file			●	●*		
Click to position		●				

*Requires keyboard qualifier

Figure 7.19
Scrolling Behavior

the entire document appears within the window. As the size of a window is reduced, components of the scroll bar can be eliminated until only the two scroll arrows remain.

OPEN LOOK places the scroll arrows at opposite ends of the scroll handle in an attempt to minimize their separation while maintaining the desirable spatial correspondence between the component parts and their directions of movement. Because the length of the scroll handle does not change to reflect the visible portion of the document, the scroll arrows remain close enough to allow easy scrolling in both directions.

During continuous scrolling, the scroll arrows move along with the scroll handle. To allow the user to avoid moving the mouse during this process, OPEN LOOK moves the mouse pointer automatically to keep it aligned with the scroll arrow. It is widely acknowledged that the user, not the system, should be allowed to exercise control of all operations. The practice of *pointer jumping* (also known as *mouse warp*), stands in apparent violation of this fundamental principle of user-centered design.

While the benefits of pointer jumping may, in this case, outweigh the costs, the disorientation that may result should be carefully evaluated before this behavior can be recommended. The placement of the scroll arrows reflects a fundamental tradeoff between clarity of representation and efficiency of human performance. The relative effectiveness of the three design solutions described above is an issue that can only be resolved experimentally.

Motif, Windows, and Presentation Manager follow the conceptual model of scrolling presented by the Macintosh by placing scroll arrows at opposite ends of scrollbar and paging by screenfulls on mouse clicks inside the scroll container. Like NextStep, these systems modify the size of the scroll handle to reflect the proportion of the document visible within the window. The keyboard can also be used to move the scroll handle incrementally in the desired direction in each of these systems. Motif adds the ability to move directly to either end of the document when mouse clicks within the scroll container are qualified by the shift (to beginning) or control (to end) keys.

Display Help Information

The Macintosh currently provides no system-level facilities for accessing online help information, although the next version, System 7.0, is intended to address this situation. Applications that need this capability must supply their own help system. While NextStep also does not provide an explicit help facility, its Digital-Librarian application provides powerful text indexing and display capabilities that can provide fast and consistent access to online documentation.

The extensive online-help facility provided by OPEN LOOK can be invoked at any time by pointing to a window or control and pressing a help key. A pop-up window then presents information associated with the specific object indicated by the mouse pointer to provide context-sensitive assistance. The help function can be mapped to any key by the user. Standard help text for the basic OPEN LOOK objects is provided in the functional specification. Users can retrieve additional, application-specific information by pressing a button labeled More in the help window.

Currently, Motif provides no standard online-help facility. Windows and Presentation Manager, in contrast, define the behavior of a standard help menu and browser window and a means of presenting them within the standard window structure. Users can pull down the help menu (using the mouse or the keyboard) to access tutorial information, help for the help system itself, or an index of available topics. Selecting an item from the menu produces a scrollable document window in which the textual help information appears.

The label for the help menu (F1=help) reminds the user that the help window can be displayed using the F1 function key. The user can also display the help window by double-clicking on the help menu title with the mouse menu button. A help button can be included in any dialogue box to provide context-sensitive access to the same window. Pressing shift with the F1 key changes the mouse pointer to a question mark and places the user in help mode. The user can then click on any object to view the related help information.

Conclusion

Because each windowing system provides different means to accomplish basic window-management tasks, each system has advantages and disadvantages. These qualities are discussed in the following section.

7.9 Advantages and Disadvantages

Introduction

Each of the six windowing systems described provides both advantages and disadvantages for users at different levels of sophistication. This chapter concludes with a capsule overview of the most important characteristics of each system.

Macintosh

The directness of interactive control provided by the Macintosh should be the goal of any windowing system. Mouse tracking is smooth and even, and objects do not lag behind the pointer during dragging operations. Even on faster, more powerful machines, none of the other systems can yet match the responsiveness and interactivity of the single-tasking Macintosh. The efficiency of the kernel-based Macintosh human interface will provide a useful benchmark for evaluating future improvements in human interfaces for more complex operating environments.

Many other performance characteristics of the Macintosh, however, are somewhat less impressive. The simple user model makes the system easy to learn but limits the flexibility available to the expert user. Particularly significant limitations include the following:

Windows can be sized from only one corner
No support for extended scrolling operations
No push window to back function
No minimize-window function
No mouseless operation
Limited keyboard control
Limited extensibility
Limited keymapping configurability

Whereas Windows and Presentation Manager are (to some extent) limited by backward compatibility with the MS-DOS environment, the Macintosh is limited by the need for compatibility with its original set of window controls and simple user model. As a result, many useful control innovations (such as the more sophisticated sizing controls provided by Windows and Presentation Manager) have not been implemented on the Macintosh.

NextStep

The apparent three-dimensional look and feel presented by NextStep is an industry trend that can be expected to continue in systems providing high-quality displays. The Display PostScript imagery produces a convincing three-dimensional effect, which enhances the impression of interaction with a real, physical environment. The responsiveness of the server-based windowing system, however, does not approach that of the Macintosh and sometimes leads to delays that reduce the directness of the user's experience.

NextStep provides the strongest orientation-oriented development tools of any of the six windowing systems. An explicit goal is the ability for even nonprogrammers to construct application-level tools from reusable software objects. In the absence of special constructions, NextStep, like the Macintosh, attempts to produce a simple interaction model that is well-suited to inexperienced users. Several negative characteristics are clearly a result of this decision:

Windows only resizable from the bottom/lower corners
No mouseless operation
Limited keyboard control

NextStep has already been licensed by IBM and can be expected to gather momentum if the initial marketing efforts in higher education are successful.

OPEN LOOK   The OPEN LOOK GUI provides the most extensive functionality of any of the systems evaluated. The power and flexibility provided for the expert user may, however, steepen the learning curve for the novice. Many of the unique features of OPEN LOOK contribute significantly to the complexity of the resulting human interface:

Complex mapping of mouse select and menu buttons
Multiple context-dependent pop-up menus (not cued)
Window selection possible without unfocusing others
Extended feedback in window, menu, and button states
Scrolling lists can be split and edited
Menu default options

Other distinguishing features of OPEN LOOK that provide useful enhancements to the basic functionality of the windowing system are more straightforward:

Proportional scaling of windows and window contents
Windows can be dragged from any border area
Move and copy text by dragging with mouse qualifier
Symbolic keyboard scrolling accelerators
Full keyboard-driven pointer navigation
Keyboard focus toggles two most recent windows
Powerful online help facility
Pattern match searching in scrolling list
Optional default to focus on window with pointer
Option to connect Notice display shadow to
origin button

Finally, OPEN LOOK displays several idiosyncratic characteristics that depart from industry standard practice. The merits of these design decisions will be a continuing topic of debate:

Pointer jumping
Scrollbar arrow placement
Keyboard shortcuts not provided for menus
Modification of look and feel prohibited
Indeterminate state information
Mouseless operation via mouse emulation

Many of the peculiarities of OPEN LOOK can be attributed to the conscious attempt at avoiding similarity in appearance and behavior to existing GUIs. The system provides access to the industry-standard X Window System and the innovative and highly extensible NeWS, as well as to the large bodies of existing software supported by each of the base windowing systems. Because of its complexity, however, OPEN LOOK may be ill-suited for nontechnical environments.

OSF/Motif

Like OPEN LOOK, the Motif Window Manager and Toolkit can leverage the efficient and proven client-server implementation provided by the X Window System. Imaging and base window services are thus tied to industry standards that can be expected to remain stable over the next several years. This fact may simplify the transition to a standardized GUI even in relatively heterogeneous hardware environments.

Like NextStep, Motif employs the three-dimensional metaphor. OSF encourages developers to create their own extensions to the basic Motif widget set. This flexibility is continued in the default behavior of the Motif Window Manager. Motif is the most permissive of the systems being compared. Among its most valuable features are:

Flexible resizing controls
Full functionality accessible from keyboard
Fully configurable mouse buttons

Keymappings can be easily modified by user
Cycle through subset of windows and window icons
Option to focus automatically on window containing
pointer

The severity of the drawbacks that do exist is reduced
by their limited number and the ease with which the
system itself can be reconfigured. Only a few criticisms
are apparent:

Nonmnemonic keyboard mappings
Limited stylistic guidance

Motif implementations gain immediate compatibility
with a large body of existing UNIX applications supporting the X Window System communication and display
protocols. For these reasons, Motif represents an ideal
choice for computing environments combining DOS-
and UNIX-based equipment.

Microsoft Windows and Presentation Manager

Apart from the differences in their underlying operating
systems and standard utilities, Windows and Presentation
Manager are largely indistinguishable in appearance and
behavior. This fact will simplify the transition as DOS
users begin to migrate to OS/2. The consistency of
Windows and Presentation Manager with the Motif
Window Manager can provide a route for future expan-
sion as well.

The joint style guide for Windows and Presentation
Manager illustrates the degree of convergence between
the two systems. These systems are distinguished (along
with Motif) by their extensive keyboard-control capabilities. Although the numerous combinations of keystrokes
and qualifiers needed for keyboard control may increase
the complexity of the human interface, Windows and
Presentation Manager provide some compensation in the
form of an easily accessed help system. These are the
only systems in which the help facility is represented explicitly in the standard window structure.

The standard controls for Windows and Presentation Manager are relatively easy to understand and should provide even inexperienced operators with an immediately usable system. The extensive use of keyboard of equivalents should, at the same time, satisfy even the most hard-core DOS user. The human-interface strengths of both Windows and Presentation Manager include:

Flexible resizing controls
Support for completely mouseless operation
Direct keyboard access for menu items
Powerful online help facility
Window shuffling using the rapid-preview option
Rapid swapping of front window and second or back window

A number of negative characteristics, however, limit the functionality of the two systems:

Nonmnemonic keyboard mappings
Keymappings cannot be modified easily by user
Some applications bypass the windowing system and take over the entire display

Windows and Presentation Manager will undoubtedly achieve market penetration comparable to that enjoyed by MS-DOS. For this reason, these systems must be considered seriously by vendors targeting executive, management, and office markets.

Conclusion   This chapter has introduced six examples of windowing systems that provide the basis for GUIs. Each commercial product offers different benefits and limitations. As they compete with each other in the market place, they are constantly changing and improving their characteristics. At this time, it is difficult to predict which will be the most successful in this decade. A better understanding of their essential characteristics, however, can help designers of GUIs to achieve better designs using the available technology.

Appendix A **Windowing-System Component Terminology**

Figure A.1 outlines some of the product-specific terminology used to describe standard components that appear in nearly all windowing systems. Cells for components with no direct equivalent in a particular system are left blank in the resulting terminology matrix.

	Macintosh	NextStep	OPEN LOOK	OSF/Motif	MS Windows	OS/2-PM
Window Types						
Window with Keyboard Focus	Active Window	Key Window	Input Area	Active Window	Active Window	Active Window
Child Window	Document Window	Standard Window	Base Window	Secondary Window	Document Window	Document Window
Modeless Dialog Box	Dialog Box	Panel	Pop-up Window	Modeless Dialog Widget	Modeless Dialog Box	Modeless Dialog Box
Modal Dialog Box	Modal Dialog Box	Attention Panel	Notice	Modal Dialog Widget	Modal Dialog Box	Modal Dialog Box
Query Box	Dialog Box	Panel	Command Window	Secondary Window	Dialog Box	Dialog Box
Message Box	Alert			Message Box	Message Box	Message Box
Window Structure						
Title Bar	Title Bar	Title Bar	Header	Title Area	Title Bar	Title Bar
Window Menu Bar			Control Area	Menu Bar	Menu Bar	Menu Bar
Message Area			Footer		Message Line	Message Line
Window Controls						
Close Control	Close Box	Close Button		System Menu Button	Control Menu Box	System Menu Box
Size Control	Size Box	Resize Button	Resize Corner	Border Resize Handle	Window Frame	Window Frame
Minimize Control		Miniaturizing Button		Minimize Button	Minimize Box	Minimize Box
Maximize Control	Zoom Box			Maximize Button	Maximize Box	Maximize Box
Restore Control	Zoom Box				Restore Box	Restore Box
Scrollbar	Scrollbar	Scroller	Scrollbar	Scrollbar	Scrollbar	Scrollbar
Scrollbar Handle	Scroll Box	Scroll Knob	Drag Area	Slider	Scroll Box	Scroll Box
Scrollbar Arrow	Scroll Arrow	Scroll Button	Arrow	Arrow	Scroll Arrow	Scroll Arrow
Menu Types						
Pull-Down Menus	Menu	Menu	Button Menu	Pull-down Menu	Drop-down Menu	Drop-down Menu
Implicit Pop-Up Menu	Pop-up Menu		Pop-up Menu	Pop-up Menu	Contextual Menu	Contextual Menu
Explicit Pop-Up Menu		Pop-up List	Button Menu			
Stay-Up Menu	Tear-off Menu	Detached Menu	Pinned Menu			

Figure A.1 Windowing-System Component Terminology

Detailed System Descriptions and Comparisons

Introduction

This appendix provides detailed comparative information for the major components of six windowing systems. The order of presentation is identical to that used in Chapter 7. Where necessary, product specific terminology is given in parentheses following a more generic term.

Windows

Overall Appearance

Each of the systems targeted at high-resolution workstation-class displays supports a simulated three-dimensional appearance. NextStep provides this visual treatment as its only style of presentation. OPEN LOOK's three-dimensional appearance characteristic is an optional feature available only on color and gray-scale displays. This appendix considers only the monochrome version. The default configuration of Motif incorporates the three-dimensional style, but the effect can be overridden for low-quality displays. The images in Figs. B.1 and B.2 document the overall appearance of the standard window in each system as well as the product-specific terminology used to identify the component parts.

Window Structure

Most windows on the Macintosh are document windows, which have a title bar and optional scrollbars along the right and bottom edges. A one-pixel black border defines the edge or edges without a scrollbar.

Macintosh

Close Box
Title Bar
Zoom Box
Scroll Box
Scroll Arrow
Size Box

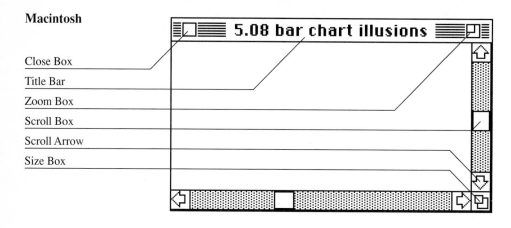

NextStep

Resize Button (2D)
Minimizing Button
Scroll Knob
Title Bar
Close Button
Scroll Buttons

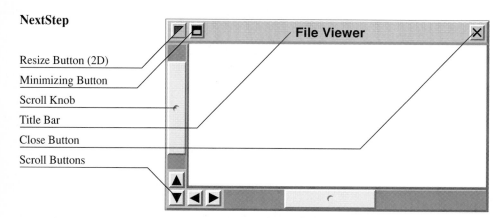

OPEN LOOK

Window Menu Button
Menu Button
Header
Drag Area
Arrow
Scroll Anchor
Footer
Resize Corner

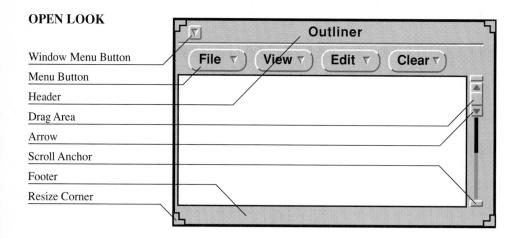

Figure B.1: Macintosh, NextStep, OPEN LOOK

Motif System

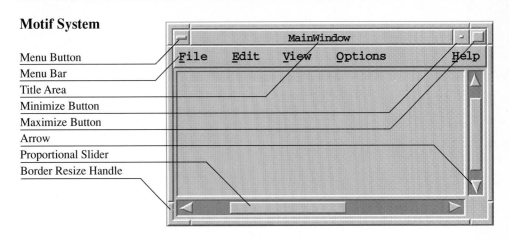

Menu Button
Menu Bar
Title Area
Minimize Button
Maximize Button
Arrow
Proportional Slider
Border Resize Handle

Microsoft Windows

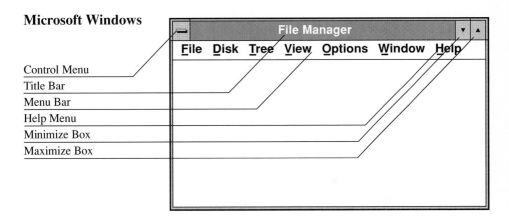

Control Menu
Title Bar
Menu Bar
Help Menu
Minimize Box
Maximize Box

OS/2 Presentation Manager

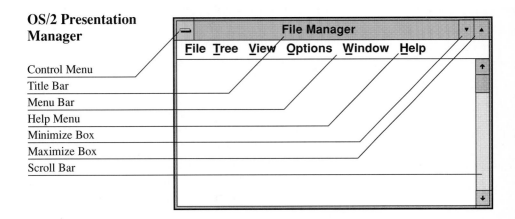

Control Menu
Title Bar
Menu Bar
Help Menu
Minimize Box
Maximize Box
Scroll Bar

Figure B.2: Motif, Windows, Presentation Manager

All document windows for a given application share a menu bar at the top of the display screen. Windows in NextStep have a title bar and optional scrollbars (Scrollers) along the left and bottom edges. By default, menus appear in the upper-left region of the display. With the appropriate preferences settings, menus can also be displayed by pressing the mouse menu button anywhere within that window.

Application windows in OPEN LOOK have a title bar (Header), a window menu button, a window border of at least two pixels, and either a control area (containing buttons or menus) or an application area. The typical OPEN LOOK application includes both; the control area separates the application area from the title bar. Optional scrollbars can be placed in control areas in the right and bottom borders. OPEN LOOK also provides an optional structural region (Footer) at the bottom of the window in which status information and short-term messages can be displayed. More permanent status messages can be displayed in the title bar.

Application windows in Motif, Windows, and Presentation Manager have a title bar and adjustable-width borders that function as controls permitting window sizing operations from any side or corner. Optional scrollbars may be included along the right or bottom edges. A menu bar is included directly beneath the title bar by most applications, but is not required. For small windows or applications with a large number of menus, the menu bar can be wrapped to produce more than one line of menu titles.

Motif windows support an optional inner border (Client Matte) of arbitrary width that visually separates the application area from the window border and provides a means of color coding the windows on display. Like OPEN LOOK, Windows and Presentation Manager permit the inclusion of an optional status display (Message Line) at the bottom of the window.

Standard Window Controls

Each of the windowing systems uses the document or application window's title bar as a handle by which the window can be positioned within the display using the mouse select button. As described in Section 7.7, some systems permit positioning using the keyboard as well. Scrollbars are provided in one or more of the window borders by each system. The following discussion reviews system-specific standard controls (see Figs. B.1 and B.2).

The standard Macintosh window (Document Window) provides a single sizing control (Size Box) in the lower-right corner. A combination maximizing and revert control (Zoom Box) at the right end of the title bar enlarges small windows to cover the entire screen and restores full-screen windows to their previous size. A close window control (Close Box) at the left end of the title bar dismisses the window and closes its associated document file.

The title bar of a NextStep window (Standard Window) contains two standard controls. At the left end is a minimize control (Miniaturizing Button), which reduces the window to an icon (Miniwindow). At the right end is a close window control (Close Button), which terminates the application or closes the document in question. Three sizing controls (Resize Buttons) are located in the bottom corners and the border separating them.

In addition to the title bar, OPEN LOOK windows can be repositioned by dragging with the mouse select button on any border region not covered by a control. The only required control is a button (Window Control Button) at the left end of the title bar providing access to a window control menu (see Section 7.4.) OPEN LOOK windows can be minimized or maximized only from this menu. Sizing controls (Resize Corners) are optional but are present by default in all four corners of OPEN LOOK application windows (Base Windows).

Motif, Windows, and Presentation Manager provide window controls that are functionally identical, even though the visual representation of some controls differs slightly in the Motif widget set (see Fig. B.2). The segmented borders of resizeable windows in all three systems provide sizing controls (Size Handles) in each corner and in all four sides. A pair of controls at the right end of the title bar permits the window to be minimized, maximized, or restored to its previous size.

Standard windows in Motif (Primary Windows), Windows, and Presentation Manager provide a window control menu (Control Menu in Windows; System Menu in Presentation Manager and Motif), which can be accessed either through a button (System Menu Box) in the left end of the title bar or from the keyboard. The same button provides a shortcut for closing the document or application associated with the window when the user double-clicks within it using the mouse select button.

Menus

Menu Appearance

The Macintosh provides a single menu bar at the top of the display screen. Its contents are the titles of pull-down submenus that present application-specific functions. The right and bottom edges of Macintosh menus are bounded by a two-pixel drop shadow to enhance the illusion of a physically distinct object floating in front of the document windows in the display. The same metaphor is used to identify undisplayed, but explicitly represented pop-up menus in Macintosh dialogue boxes.

The currently selected item in a Macintosh menu is highlighted using inverse video in monochrome systems and a user-specified highlight color in systems supporting color displays. Items with attached submenus have a rightward-pointing arrow at the right edge of the menu. Keyboard shortcuts also appear at the right edge of the menu and are represented by the symbol for the Apple command key and the keyboard character that implements the shortcut.

Menus in NextStep adopt the same three-dimensional appearance characteristics displayed by other NextStep components. Each menu has its own title bar, which contains the name of the menu and a minimizing control (Minimize Button) permitting the menu to be reduced to an icon. As users navigate through the menu system, the highlight and shadow regions at the edges of the selected item are reversed to create the illusion that the button has been pushed into the display. To increase the perceptual salience of the selected item, its background color is changed from light gray to white.

The command key used to access all NextStep keyboard shortcuts is not explicitly represented within the menu itself. Because the command key is implied for all shortcuts, only the alphanumeric character appears at the right end of the menu item as a reminder for the user. An uppercase letter implies both the shift key and the command key.

Pulldown menus in OPEN LOOK are attached to buttons and are denoted by a downward-facing pointer. Submenus and explicit pop-up menus replace the downward-facing pointer with one facing to the right. The menu itself incorporates a six-pixel wide drop shadow to provide visual separation from the display. Implicit pop-up menus include the menu title at the top of the list of items, but are otherwise comparable to those menus attached to buttons.

OPEN LOOK menus and dialogue boxes that can be kept on display a side-view image of a pushpin (in the upper left corner, see Fig. B.1) when not being explicitly retained. When the user clicks the mouse select button on this control (Pushpin), the original image is replaced by an end view making the pushpin appear to be pushed into the surface of the display (see Fig. B.1).

When an OPEN LOOK menu is displayed, its default selection is indicated by a button-shaped outline around the menu item. As the user navigates through the menu, the currently selected item is surrounded by a button-shaped colored or inverted region (see Fig. 7.9). Unlike the other systems, OPEN LOOK does not provide keyboard shortcuts for menu items.

Menus in Motif appear as lists on the surface of a flat panel. The edges of the panel are distinguished by the three-dimensional appearance treatment applied throughout the Motif widget set. As in NextStep, a three-dimensional manipulation is applied to the selected menu item as well. The background color of both the menu title and the currently selected item is changed, but the highlight and shadow applied by Motif makes the selected item appear to be raised, rather than lowered.

Menus in Windows and Presentation Manager identify the currently selected menu item by inverting the item or replacing its background with the current highlight color. Each of the item names may contain a single underlined character that identifies a key by which that item can be selected directly from the keyboard while the menu is on display. Keyboard shortcuts are identified at the right end of the menu item using three-letter abbreviations for the necessary qualifier keys.

Menu Behavior

Menus on the Macintosh are displayed when the user points to an item in the menu bar and presses the mouse button. The menu remains on display until the user releases the mouse button. Up to five levels of cascading, hierarchical submenus may be incorporated. Submenus are displayed whenever the item to which they are linked in the parent menu is selected.

Stay-up (Tear-off) menus can be pulled from the menu bar and placed anywhere within the display by dragging the mouse pointer across the edge of the menu without making a selection. An outline of the menu provides feedback as it is dragged into position and placed by releasing the mouse button. Explicit pop-up menus appear in control panels and are displayed to the right of the button to which they are attached.

Menus in NextStep are presented in the upper-left corner of the display and remain visible until the associated application is terminated. In the standard configuration, interaction with these stay-up menus is accomplished using the mouse select button. A user-preferences setting allows the mouse menu button to automatically summon an implicit, window-specific pop-up menu by clicking or pressing anywhere within a window. NextStep menus appear in front of any application or document windows and cannot be moved behind other objects.

When displayed by clicking, NextStep menus follow the stay-up model and remain on display until explicitly dismissed by the user. When displayed by pressing, the standard pop-up menu behavior is exhibited. The behavior of submenus follows the same convention. Stay-up submenus (invoked by clicking, rather than pressing) are dismissed by clicking in the item in the parent menu to which they are attached. Stay-up submenus can be detached from their parent menu and positioned independently. When detached, an additional control (Close Button) appears at the right end of the menu's title bar and allows the menu to be dismissed by the user.

Both pulldown and pop-up menus are also employed by OPEN LOOK. Pulldown menus are attached to buttons in the window control area directly beneath the title bar. Explicit pop-up menus may be attached to buttons appearing in any control area or dialogue box. Implicit pop-up menus associated with various window regions and controls can be displayed by pressing the mouse menu button anywhere within the region.

As in NextStep, OPEN LOOK menus can be invoked by either clicking or pressing the mouse menu button. In either case, however, the menu disappears as soon as the user makes a selection or clicks beyond the menu boundaries. Stay-up (Pinned) menus must be explicitly retained by clicking or pressing the mouse select button on a control (Pushpin) in the upper-left corner of the menu. Unlike the other systems, OPEN LOOK displays submenus only when the mouse pointer moves into the rightmost area of a menu item to which a submenu is attached.

Like OPEN LOOK, Motif incorporates separate pull-down and pop-up menu systems. Both the press-drag-release and the click-position-click protocols are supported. By default, the mouse select button is used to manipulate menus in Motif. Pulldown menus can appear within windows and an implicit pop-up menu (Workspace Menu) is available from outside any window. User- or application-defined items can be attached to the mouse menu button and accessed as implicit pop-up menus. Hierarchical submenus can be added to any menu item.

Windows and Presentation Manager also support both pulldown and pop-up menus. The mouse select button is used for all menu operations. The Microsoft style guide recommends using only one level of hierarchical submenus, but the windowing system does not enforce this limit. Menus can be displayed by either clicking or pressing, but stay-up menus are not described in the style guide.

Behavior at Boundaries

Macintosh menus that are too long (vertically) to fit within the display screen are automatically scrolled to reveal items beyond the borders of the display. Whenever the user drags the mouse pointer beyond the end of the full-length menu, the previously obscured items scroll by in the opposite direction. Menus that exceed the height of the screen are typically needed only for items such as font names, where the number of entries cannot be predicted by the developer.

Menus in NextStep are displayed consistently beneath and to the right of the mouse pointer, regardless of the screen location. Menus that extend beyond the borders of the display are clipped at the edge of the screen. OPEN LOOK menus in the same situation are adjusted to fit within the display. The menu or submenu is shifted left far enough to allow the entire menu to appear within the display. Border-region menu behavior in Motif, Windows, and Presentation Manager is application dependent. Pulldown menus that do not fit within the application window in these systems are displayed in the opposite direction above and outside the window.

Window Control Menus

The Macintosh assumes that window-management operations will be performed using the window controls. The only window control operation available from the menu system simply closes the active window. The operation is embedded in the standard file menu (see Application menus subsection) and is presented to the user as a document operation rather than a window operation. NextStep also provides limited access to window control functions in the standard application menu system. Users can minimize, size, or close windows from the standard window menu (which is comparable to the Macintosh File menu).

Each of the remaining systems provides a menu separated physically from the application-menu system, which is dedicated exclusively to window control operations. The standard operations provided by each of these menus permit windows to be minimized, maximized, or restored to their previous size.

For application windows, OPEN LOOK presents window control functions in a menu attached to a required control (Window Menu Button) at the left end of the title bar. The basic operations (minimize, maximize, restore) are supplemented by options to push the window to the back of the stack (Back), end the application (Quit), and redraw the display (Refresh). A different window control menu is required for OPEN LOOK child (Pop-up) windows. The child-window control menu provides options to close the window (Dismiss), push the window back (Back), redraw the display (Refresh), and identify the parent window (Owner).

The Motif window control menu (System Menu) is accessed through a button at the left end of the title bar. The menu is displayed by clicking or dragging on this control (System Menu Box), or by pressing the alternate key followed by the space bar (which is the object represented by the bar-shaped symbol on the button itself). In addition to the standard operations, the Motif window control menu allows users to move, size, or close the window, or to push it to the back of the display (Lower). The window control menu for the active window can also be displayed by pressing the mouse select button outside of any other window.

The window control menu in both Windows (Control Menu) and Presentation Manager (System Menu) is essentially identical to that seen in Motif. The only difference is the replacement of Motif's window-to-back option with a command (Task Manager) allowing the user to switch easily between application windows.

Window control menus in Windows and Presentation Manager, like those in Motif, can be accessed using either the mouse or the alternate key and spacebar.

Component Menus

Four additional standard menu types are defined by OPEN LOOK. The standard menus (see Fig. B.1) support system-level functions and are required in any conforming application. All of these additional menus are implicit pop-up menus associated with a particular component or region of the display and can be summoned by pressing the mouse menu button within the appropriate area.

The OPEN LOOK settings menu is attached to component-specific control panels (Property Windows). This menu can be displayed by pressing the mouse menu button anywhere within the interior of the application window and used to clear, initialize, or apply the settings. Pressing the mouse menu button outside of any window invokes a workspace menu, which allows users to change their preferences settings, launch application and utility programs, or exit the windowing system.

The scroll bar and scrolling list menus are implicit pop-up menus that appear when the mouse menu button is clicked or pressed within controls of the corresponding type. The menus extend the basic functionality of the control and provide a means for incorporating application-specific features. The standard menu types must be supported by any application being certified for conformance to the OPEN LOOK functional specification. Only the scrollbar and scrolling list menus can be modified by the application.

Application Menus

Virtually all Macintosh application menu bars begin
with the standard Apple command, file, and edit
menus. The Apple command menu launches subpro-
grams (Desk Accessories) and provides information
about the application, while the file and edit menus
present commands for common file system and editing
functions that function transparently across applications. Application-specific menu items may be added to
the standard contents of these menus, and additional
menus may be appended to the menu bar. The first
three items of standard NextStep application menus are
the info, window, and edit submenus, the contents of
which are comparable to the three standard menus on
the Macintosh.

In addition to the required window control menu, the
style guide for OPEN LOOK suggests standard file,
view, edit, and properties menus attached to buttons in
the control area separating the application area from the
menu bar. The view menu provides options controlling
the way data is displayed. The properties menu is used
to display and change the attributes associated with the
currently selected object. Only the standard window
control menu is provided in the default configuration of
the Motif Window Manager, but this configuration can
be easily modified by creating appropriate (ASCII) resource files. Application developers and even end users
are expected to customize the menu-bar contents and
the mouse-button mappings to meet their own particular needs.

The standard application menus recommended by the
Windows and Presentation Manager style guide are the
control (System, in Presentation Manager), file, edit,
view, window, and help menus. The control menu is
the window control menu described above. The file,
edit, and view menus are comparable to those discussed
previously. The window menu is used by applications

supporting multiple document windows to provide a list of open windows and a means of switching between them. The style guide recommends providing an automatic window arrangement option in this menu. The help menu is always located at the extreme right end of the menu bar and provides a list of entry points for the help system.

Default Menu Selections

Default selections allow the user to select frequently needed items from menus without navigating through the menu and correctly positioning the mouse pointer. As might be expected from their orientation toward a simple user model, Macintosh and NextStep do not support default menu selections at any level. The mechanism supplied by OPEN LOOK, in contrast, permits the user to specify a default selection for any menu or submenu. When a menu first appears, the default item is identified by a button-shaped outline that disappears as soon as the pointer is moved into the menu to select a different item.

An OPEN LOOK menu's default selection can be viewed without displaying the menu by pressing the mouse select button within the object to which the menu is attached. The default item name appears directly to the right of the rightward-facing arrow or directly beneath the downward-facing arrow and can be accepted immediately by releasing the mouse button. Clicking the mouse select button in the object to which the menu is attached selects the default option without displaying the menu or the default item. The first item in the menu is the default selection if no other item has been specified. Default selections for implicit pop-up menus are invoked by double-clicking with the mouse menu button in any area from which the menu can be summoned.

Motif, Windows, and Presentation Manager all provide a limited default capability, but the option is available only for the help and window control (System) menus and cannot be modified by the user. Double-clicking the mouse select button on the window control menu selects the option (Close) that closes the window. In Windows and Presentation Manager, double-clicking on the help menu title bypasses the help menu and displays a dedicated help window.

Controls and Dialogue Boxes

Standard Controls

Each of the windowing systems implements several types of command buttons, inclusive and exclusive settings, proportional sliders, scrolling lists, and individual fields for textual and numeric data. The Macintosh human interface utilizes a set of predefined (Toolbox) routines to implement this basic set of controls. Specialized controls are rarely seen on the Macintosh, primarily because of the ease with which applications can make use of the standard control definitions in the Macintosh ROM.

A comparable suite of rudimentary controls is supplied by NextStep, but the basic components can be modified more easily than those in the standard Macintosh environment. NextStep provides an object-oriented development environment (Application Kit) that allows new controls to be defined by creating instances of objects in a class library that implements the standard controls, windows, and other NextStep components.

The standard OPEN LOOK control set is defined more extensively than that of any of its competitors. The basic control set is enhanced by options providing specialized behavior and extended functionality for most of the standard control types. Unlike the other windowing systems, OPEN LOOK does not permit modifications to the appearance and behavior of the standard controls in certified implementations.

- All OPEN LOOK components (windows, dialogues, controls, etc.) represent state information using the same conventions. The state of any control may be selected, active, indeterminate, or inactive. In general, the representations of these states correspond to decreasing levels of perceptual salience. Indeterminate and inactive controls, for example, are reduced in contrast by replacing solid and double lines with dotted and patterned lines.

OPEN LOOK scrollbars and scrolling lists can be split, edited in place, and operated through implicit pop-up menus. A pattern-matching feature immediately selects the first matching item in a scrolling list as the user enters characters from the keyboard. Hierarchical scrolling lists employ explicit representations (Glyphs) for the presence of additional levels as well as the depth within the hierarchy of the current level.

Other specialized OPEN LOOK characteristics include single-line text fields that can be scrolled in place to provide space for additional entries, scrollbars that shed components as the length of their container is reduced, and untitled minimal (Abbreviated) buttons (such as the button for the standard window control menu) providing only the symbol for the type of object (menu, control panel, etc.) attached to the button.

Motif provides a simple widget set incorporating all the basic controls. Because of the object-oriented design of the Motif widget set, the appearance and behavior of the basic control set can be extended as necessary by the developer. OSF has, in fact, encouraged developers to create their own proprietary widget sets to allow product differentiation within the context of the structural and behavioral consistency provided by the Motif Window Manager.

In Windows and Presentation Manager, the basic control types are supplemented by a variety of drop-down lists and combination list-and-text field controls. The drop-down lists are similar to pulldown menus but can appear anywhere within the dialogue box or application window. Both systems also specify a protocol for manipulating any of the standard controls entirely from the keyboard. Like OPEN LOOK, Windows and Presentation Manager provide pattern matching to enhance keyboard selection from scrolling lists. Other controls are selected with the tab key and manipulated using the spacebar and arrow keys.

Button Vocabulary

Command buttons cause actions to be initiated immediately by the system. One or more command buttons are always provided in any dialogue box to allow the user to end the dialogue and dismiss the child window in which it appears. The following discussion describes the visual conventions used by each system to provide information about the buttons themselves (see Fig. 7.9).

The Macintosh identifies the default button for a dialogue box by placing a four-pixel border around the perimeter of the button. Disabled buttons are dimmed, and selected buttons highlighted, in the same way as Macintosh menu items (by graying and inverting, respectively). As in the menu system, an ellipsis signifies the presence of an attached dialogue box. The default button in NextStep dialogue boxes is identified by a symbol representing the return key. The labels of disabled buttons are printed in gray instead of black. Like selected NextStep menu items, selected buttons change from light gray to white and appear to be recessed into the surface of the control panel.

Buttons in OPEN LOOK, like other objects in this system, provide visual representations of their current state. The solid background of a command button, for example, is replaced with a gray pattern while the command is executing (Busy). Labels for buttons that are disabled are grayed and selected buttons are inverted. As in the Macintosh, an ellipsis indicates an attached dialogue box. An upward- or downward-facing pointer indicates an attached menu. The Motif Toolkit specification also defines a standard button vocabulary. These buttons are shown in Fig. 7.9

Windows and Presentation Manager represent the default button by increasing the width of the button border. When navigating through a dialogue box from the keyboard, the currently selected command button is identified by a one-pixel dotted line surrounding the button label. Mnemonic characters providing direct keyboard access to specific command buttons are underlined as in the menu system.

Pointer Jumping

A unique dialogue-management feature provided by OPEN LOOK is the automatic positioning of the mouse pointer on the default button of control panels and query or message boxes. If the user clicks to accept the default without moving the mouse out of the but ton area, the pointer is returned to its previous location when the dialogue box disappears. Otherwise, the pointer remains in its new location. A comparable technique is used to simplify the operation of OPEN LOOK scrollbars. The pointer is automatically repositioned to remain on the scroll arrow when scrolling by lines and in front of the scroll handle when paging by window-sized chunks. Either of these behaviors (Pointer Jumping) can be disabled through a user preferences setting.

Dialogue-Box Types

Stylistic conventions for dialogue boxes (control panels, query boxes, and message boxes) are described by each of the windowing systems except Motif. The following discussion reviews major differences in appearance and behavior for control panels, query boxes, and message boxes across windowing systems.

The Macintosh defines both modal and modeless dialogue boxes. Modal dialogue boxes have a double line
around their outermost border and appear in the center
of the display. Modeless dialogues have a standard
Macintosh title bar with which they can be freely repositioned. Modeless dialogues may also incorporate the
standard window close control in place of an explicit
cancel option in the dialogue itself. Macintosh control
panels and query boxes are implemented as either modal or modeless dialogue boxes. Message boxes (Alerts)
are modal dialogue boxes in which the user can
respond only by clicking buttons or pressing return or
enter to accept the default selection.

Modeless dialogue boxes (Panels) in NextStep have the
same title bar as standard windows, permitting them to
be dragged to any position in the display. The title bar
may contain controls for minimizing and closing the
panel as well. Modal dialogue boxes (Attention Panels)
cannot be moved, minimized, or covered by any window. Modal dialogues are identified by a solid black
title bar containing no text or controls. They remain on
display even after the associated application or document has been minimized.

Three types of dialogue box are defined by the OPEN
LOOK functional specification. Modeless dialogue
boxes share the basic window structure and serve as
control panels for issuing commands with multiple
parameters (Command Windows) and for setting attributes of standard OPEN LOOK objects (Property
Windows). Both classes provide a control (Pushpin)
allowing them to be attached to a particular area of the
display. Message boxes (Notices) are modal dialogue
boxes with a two-pixel border and an optional graphic
device (Shadow) that makes the message box appear to
project forward in space. The shadow emphasizes the
modal dialogue box and visually links it to the button
causing it to appear.

Dialogue boxes in Motif, Windows, and Presentation Manager may be modeless, application semimodal, application modal, or system modal. Application modal dialogues prevent further operations within the application generating the dialogue, but other tasks are not blocked. Application semimodal dialogues permit only limited operations within the application with which they are associated. System modal dialogues, in contrast, must receive a response from the user before action can be taken on any process.

All dialogue boxes in these systems are nonresizeable. Movable dialogue boxes have a standard title bar and a window control menu containing only the move and close commands. Modal dialogue boxes are indicated by a bold inner border. In addition to the standard dialogue types, the Microsoft style guide describes special control panels (Expanded Dialogue Boxes) that can be expanded in the rightward or downward direction to present specialized or advanced controls without confusing inexperienced users.

Special command buttons that facilitate navigation between related control panels are also documented by the style guide. Goto buttons dismiss the current control panel and open a related panel, while gosub buttons open the related panel without dismissing the current panel. When the new control panel is dismissed, the user is returned automatically to the previous panel.

Mouse and Keyboard Interface

Mouse-Button Mappings

The Macintosh human interface is designed around the use of a one-button mouse. As a result, the user's model of the system is simplified, but the reduction in contextual information limits the operations that can be performed with the mouse alone. Implicit pop-up menus, for example, are of limited value (unless invoked through a keyboard qualifier key) because the mouse cannot be used to select or manipulate anything within the region associated with the pop-up menu.

NextStep employs a two-button mouse. In the default configuration, either button may be used for any mouse operation and implicit pop-up menus are not available. As an alternative, one of the mouse buttons may be configured to display the menu for any window in which it is clicked or pressed. This option can be set and the mapping of the mouse select and menu buttons matched to the handedness of the user in the preferences control panel.

OPEN LOOK is designed to work with a one-, two-, or three-button mouse. When fewer than three buttons are available, keyboard qualifiers (that is, Shift and Control) are used to invoke the menu and adjust functions. Four other mouse operations are always accessed through keyboard qualifiers, which are created by mapping four symbolic functions to physical keys.

Pressing the modifier key D while dragging the mouse on a selected object creates and drags a copy of that object rather than the object itself. A special key (Constrain) limits pointer motion to the horizontal or vertical axis whenever it is depressed during a dragging operation. Another special key (Pan) effectively substitutes the moving data model of scrolling behavior for the moving window model by allowing the user to drag the contents with the mouse.

Each of these functions is commonly available as application-dependent behavior in other systems. Their implementation at the system level in OPEN LOOK ensures universal availability and consistent access. Finally, a specific function (Setmenudefault) identifies a particular menu item as the default selection when the menu button is double-clicked. It has no equivalent in any of the other systems.

Mice with as many as five buttons can be understood by the Motif Window Manager. The default mappings make use of only the leftmost button, with the remaining buttons available for application- or user-specified operations. The default behavior can be modified by the user and any of the available operations can be mapped to any combination of mouse button actions.

Windows and Presentation Manager assume a two-button mouse, but require only one of the buttons for any windowing system operation. The second button can be used by applications to abort or cancel operations. As in NextStep, the user can reverse the mapping of the buttons through a preferences setting. The third button, when present, is reserved for application-specified operations.

Keyboard Focus

The Macintosh represents the active window by completely rendering the window controls and the horizontal line pattern in the title bar. Inactive windows display only the window title and the outlines of the window, title bar, and scroll bars. The active window (Key Window) in NextStep is indicated by changing the title bar from medium gray to black. When a dialogue box appears in front of the active window, the title bar of that window (Main Window) changes from black to dark gray as the dialogue receives the keyboard focus.

In OPEN LOOK, the window with the keyboard focus is identified by a title bar that is highlighted by changing its background to black or to a special highlight color. A window for which input is temporarily blocked (Busy Window) is represented by a title bar with a patterned gray background. OPEN LOOK is the only system that does not require some window or icon to own the keyboard focus at all times. Clicking the mouse select button outside any window detaches the keyboard.

In Motif, Windows, and Presentation Manager, the window with the keyboard focus is identified by the color of its title bar. Motif provides the option of installing a window-specific color map that modifies the colors of the entire display as well as those of the newly focused window.

Keyboard Menu Shortcuts

Macintosh and NextStep users invoke keyboard short-cuts by simultaneously pressing a dedicated command key and the specified alphanumeric key. The shift or alternate keys may be used in conjunction with the command key as qualifiers. OPEN LOOK permits key-board accelerators to be defined and managed by an application, but prohibits the display of the character equivalents within the menus themselves. OPEN LOOK also permits accelerators for default and cancel options in any dialogue box, but these shortcuts are also hidden from the user. Motif, Windows, and Presentation Manager use the alternate key in conjunction with alphanumeric or function keys to implement keyboard shortcuts for menu selections. The key serving as the accelerator and the required qualifiers are listed at the right end of each menu item. Motif permits keyboard accelerators only for items in the window control menu. Windows and Presentation Manager, however, permit any menu item to take advantage of this capability.

Keyboard Menu Navigation

Unlike keyboard shortcuts, which do not display the menu, keyboard navigation allows menus to be visually traversed in a manner analogous to mouse navigation. Neither the Macintosh nor NextStep permit menu navigation from the keyboard. The standard emulation of mouse behavior provided by OPEN LOOK allows menu navigation using the arrow keys and the mouse-button keyboard equivalents.

The keyboard can be used to navigate the menu system in Motif, Windows, and Presentation Manager. The alternate key (Menu Access Button) is pressed to place the user in menu navigation mode. The arrow keys can then be used to step through the menu items and the return key to accept the currently selected item. If direct access character equivalents (see Fig. 7.4) are specified for the items in the currently displayed menu, the appropriate alphanumeric key can be typed in lieu of arrow and return key presses to invoke the desired item.

One useful aspect of the direct character-access design feature is the capability for typing ahead of the menu display and the possibility that menu-access characters can be combined into meaningful higher-level units that can be remembered and typed as "words." A new (Empty) document window, for example, can be opened in Presentation Manager by typing "fn" while holding down the alternate key to activate in succession the keyboard menu navigation mode, the file menu, and the new option.

Keyboard Control Operation

Each of the systems being compared provides at least limited keyboard operation of controls by using the tab key to step from text field to text field in a dialogue box and the return key to accept the default option. In the Macintosh and NextStep, these operations are the only ones provided. This limited support is extended by OPEN LOOK, which permits keyboard manipulation of scrollbars through logical keyboard functions for scrolling by line or by page and for moving directly to either end of a document.

Keyboard control operation is possible in Motif, but the functional specification does not describe a standard implementation. Windows and Presentation Manager provide a keyboard scrolling protocol comparable to that seen in OPEN LOOK when the cursor has been placed at the window edge opposite the direction in which the window contents are to be scrolled. The page up, page down, home, end, or arrow keys are then used to accomplish the necessary scrolling. Scrolling lists are manipulated in the same way.

Windows and Presentation Manager also support keyboard navigation through dialogue boxes using the tab key and spacebar. Any of the controls in a dialogue box can be manipulated using the keyboard alone. A one-pixel dotted line (Cursor) identifies the currently affected component. The tab key is used to move between groups of controls and the spacebar is used to set individual items such as check boxes and radio buttons. Pressing the enter key at any time accepts the default response (normally a command button) for the dialogue. As the keyboard cursor is moved through the command buttons (using the arrow keys), the response attached to the enter key becomes the button containing the cursor.

Conclusion

This appendix has provided detailed comparative information about the six windowing systems reviewed in Chapter 7.

Acknowledgments

The chapter sections are revised versions of the following articles.

Chapter 1 Layout

1.1 Proportion and Grids: Invisible Keys to Successful Layout

An edited version of "Invisible Guide Stands Behind Good Layouts," *Computer Graphics Today* 3, no. 6, June/July, 1986, p. 7ff., published by Media Horizons, Inc., New York, reprinted with permission.

1.2 Graphic Design of Spatial Metaphors, Displays, and Tools

An edited version of "Spatial Displays and Tools in Computer Graphics," *Computer Graphics Today* 5, no. 1, January 1988, pp. 26ff., published by Media Horizons, New York, reprinted with permission.

1.3 An Annotated Bibliography for Graphic Design of Spatial Displays

An edited version of "Guides to Spatial Depth Cues and Spatial Form Can Help the Designer of User Interfaces and Information Graphics," *Computer Graphics Today* 5, no. 3, March 1988, pp. 24ff., published by Media Horizons, Inc., New York, reprinted with permission. This section is also based on the author's conference article "Spatial User Interface Design Issues from the Graphic Designer's Perspective" in

Ellis, Stephen R., ed., *Proceedings Spatial Displays and Spatial Instruments Conference*, pub. no.10032, NASA Ames Research Center, Moffett Field, CA, 1989, sponsored by NASA Ames Research Center and the University of California at Berkeley, 31 August 1987, Asilomar, California. Available through Stephen R. Ellis, Mail Stop 239-3, NASA Ames Research Center, Moffett Field, CA 94035.

**Chapter 2
Typography**

2.1 Making Type Decisions

An edited reprint of "Display Users Now Making Type Decisions," *Computer Graphics Today* 1, no. 3, September 1984, pp. 18ff., published by Media Horizons Inc., New York, reprinted with permission.

2.2 Forms Design

An edited version of "Design Tips for Winning Forms," in *Computer Graphics Today* 5, no. 1, November 1988, pp. 27ff., published by Media Horizons, Inc. New York, reprinted with permission, also "Self Fulfilling Forms," *Publish!* 5, no. 8, 1988, pp. 57-63.

2.3 The Typography of Complex Documentation: Computer Programs

An edited version of "Programmers Begin to Reap Graphics Fruit," *Computer Graphics Daily,* May 1986, a special issue of *Computer Graphics Today*, published by Media Horizons, Inc., New York, reprinted with permission.

Chapter 3 Symbolism

3.1 Clarity and Consistency in Icon Design

An edited version of "Icon Design Requires Clarity and Consistency," *Computer Graphics Today* 1, no. 5, November 1984, pp. 7ff., published by Media Horizons, Inc., New York, reprinted with permission.

3.2 Icon Design Tips

An edited version of "Tips for Icon Design" *Computer Graphics Today* 6, no. 1, January 1989, pp. 24ff. Published by Media Horizons, Inc., reprinted with permission.

3.3 Icon Design in a CAD/CAM Graphical User Interface: A Case Study

An edited version of "A Good CAD/CAM User Interface is no Accident," *Computer Graphics Today* 4, no. 3, March 1987, pp. 30ff. Published by Media Horizons, Inc., New York, reprinted with permission.

3.4 An Annotated Bibliography of Signs, Icons, and Symbols

An edited version of "Computer Iconographics: Readings of Signs, "*Computer Graphics Today* 4, No.7, July 1987, pp.19-20. Published by Media Horizons, Inc., New York, reprinted with permission.

Chapter 4 Color

4.1 The Ten Commandments of Color

An edited version of "Users Must Establish Own Rules for Color," *Computer Graphics Today* 2, no. 9, September 1985, pp. 7ff., published by Media Horizons, Inc. New York, reprinted with permission.

Chapter 5 Visualizing Knowledge: Charts, Diagrams, and Maps

5.1 Chart Design

An edited version of "Business Users Need Design Knowledge," *Computer Graphics Today* 1, no. 7, November 1985, pp. 21ff., published by Media Horizons, Inc., New York, reprinted with permission.

5.3 An Annotated Bibliography of Map Design

An edited version of "Classic Cartography Readings," *Computer Graphics Today* 4, no. 11, published by Media Horizons, Inc., New York, reprinted with permission.

Chapter 6
Screen Design for
User Interfaces

6.1 Common User-Interface Design

Edited version of *Common User Interface Design: The Kodak Approach*, no. A8D027, Eastman Kodak Company, Rochester, NY, May 1988, reprinted with permission.

6.2 The User-Interface Standards Manual as a Tool for Effective Management

An edited version of "The User Interface Standards Manual: A Tool for Effective Management," *Proceedings, NCGA Computer Graphics '87 Eighth Annual Conference and Exposition*, Technical Sessions Vol. 3, published by the National Computer Graphics Association, Fairfax, VA, 1987, pp. 461-479.

Chapter 7
A Comparison of
Graphical User
Interfaces

This chapter is an edited version of a similarly titled report prepared in cooperation with Ron Zeno and Georges Merx of the Human Interface Technology Group, Application Environment Products, Systems Engineering-San Diego, NCR Corporation, San Diego, California. Reprinted with the permission of NCR Corporation. ©1990 Copyright by NCR Corporation and Aaron Marcus and Associates. The author acknowledges the assistance of former staff member Kevin Mullet in the preparation of this text.

This section appeared in an edited version in "Graphical User Interface Comparison," ACM/SIGCHI-90 Tutorial Notes, pp. 67-107, prepared by Aaron Marcus and Associates, published by ACM/SIGCHI, New York.

Design and Editing The book design is by Aaron Marcus and Associates. Programs used: Adobe Illustrator 3.0, Adobe Photoshop, Aldus PageMaker 4.0, Aldus Freehand 2.02, AppleScan, Microsoft Word 4.0, SuperPaint 2.0A.

The author would like to acknowledge the following current and former staff members for their assistance with the preparation of this book:

David Collier, Text editing
N. Gregory Galle, Text editing and layout
Grant Letz, Image editing and layout
Sherry Markwart, Text editing
Kevin Mullet, Text and image editing of Chapter 7
Sandra Ragan, Image editing, layout, and cover
June Simonsen, Text editing
Bernadette C. Tyler, Technical text editing

Acknowledgment is also due to the following persons who facilitated the publishing of this book:

Janet Benton, ACM Press, New York
Peter Gordon, Addison-Wesley Publishing Company, Reading, Massachusetts

Finally, thanks are due to the following publishing firms and organizations that permitted reprinting of articles originally appearing in their publications:

Association for Computing Machinery (ACM)/
Special Interest Group on Human-Computer Interaction (SIGCHI)
Addison-Wesley Publishing Company
Prime Computervision
Eastman Kodak Company
Media Horizons, Inc.
NCR Corporation
National Computer Graphics Association (NCGA)
NASA, Ames Research Center

Bibliography

1.1 Proportion and Grids: Invisible Keys to Successful Layout

American Institute of Graphic Arts, *Symbol Signs*, Visual Communication Books, Hastings House, New York, 1981, ISBN 0-8038-6777-8.

Baecker, Ron, and Aaron Marcus, "Design Principles for the Enhanced Presentation of Computer Program Source Text," *Proc., Conference on Human Factors in Computing Systems* (SIGCHI '86), Boston, April 1986, pp. 51-58.

Baecker, Ron, and Aaron Marcus, *Human Factors and Typography for More Readable Programs*, Addison-Wesley Publishing Co., 1990.

Ghyka, Matila, *The Geometry of Art and Life,* Sheed and Ward, New York, 1946.

Hartley, James, *Designing Instructional Text*, Nichols Publishing Co., New York, 1978.

Hurlburt, Allen, *Publication Design*, revised edition, Van Nostrand Reinhold Co., New York, 1976.

Marcus, Aaron, and Ron Baecker, "On the Graphic Design of Program Text," *Proc., Graphics Interface '82*, National Computer Graphics Associates of Canada, Toronto, 1982, 302-311. (Also published as Lawrence Berkeley Laboratory tech., report LBL 14810, University of California, May 1982)

Mueller-Brockman, Josef, *Grid Systems in Graphic Design*, Verlag Arthur Niggli, Niederteufen, Switzerland, 1981.

Stevens, Peter S., *Handbook of Regular Patterns: An Introduction to Symmetry in Two Dimensions*, MIT Press, Cambridge, 1981.

White, Jan V., *Editing by Design*, 2d ed., R. R. Bowker Company, New York, 1982.

1.2 Graphic Design of Spatial Metaphors, Displays, and Tools

Berkman, Aaron, *Art and Space,* Social Sciences, New York, 1949, 175 pp.

Bolt, Richard A., *The Human Interface: Where People and Computers Meet,* Lifetime Learning Publications, Wadsworth, California, 113 pp.

Critchlow, Keith, *Order in Space: A Design Source Book,* Studio Book, Viking Press, New York, 1970, 120 pp.

Ghyka, Matila, *The Geometry of Art and Life,* Sheed and Ward, New York, 1946, 174 pp.

Gould, Laura, and William Finzer, *Programming by Rehearsal,* Xerox Palo Alto Research Center Technical Report SCL-84-1, May, 1984, 133 pp. Also a shorter version in *Byte,* vol. 9, no. 6, June 1984.

Gregory, R. L., *The Intelligent Eye,* McGraw-Hill, New York, 1970, 191 pp.

—— *Eye and Brain: The Psychology of Seeing,* World University Library, McGraw-Hill, New York, 1968, 251 pp.

Hall, Edward T., *The Hidden Dimension,* Anchor Books, New York, 1982, 217 pp.

—— *The Silent Language,* Fawcett World Library, New York, 1963, 192 pp.

Hambidge, Jay, *The Elements of Dynamic Symmetry,* Dover Publications, New York, 1967, 133 pp.

Herdeg, Walter, *ed., Graphis Diagrams,* Graphis Press, Zurich, 1981, 205 pp.

Industrial Design Magazine, published by Design Publications, Inc., New York.

Ivins, William M., Jr., *Art and Geometry: A Study in Space Intuitions,* Dover Publications, New York, 1946, 113 pp.

Jencks, Charles, and William Chaitkin, *Architecture Today*, Harry N. Abrams, New York, 1982.

Lakoff, George, and Mark Johnson, *Metaphors We Live By,* The University of Chicago Press, Chicago, 1984, 242 pp.

Loran, Erle, *Cézanne's Composition: Analysis of His Form with Diagrams and Photographs of His Motifs,* University of California Press, Berkeley, 1963, 143 pp.

March, Lionel, and Philip Steadman, *The Geometry of Environment: An Introduction to Spatial Organization in Design,* RIBA Publications, London, 1971, 360 pp.

Marcus, Aaron, et al., "Screen Design Guidelines," *Proc.* National Computer Graphics Association Annual Conference and Exposition, 14-18 April 1985, 105-137 pp.

—— "Corporate Identity for Iconic Interface Design: The Graphic Design Perspective," *IEEE Computer Graphics and Applications,* vol. 4, no. 7, IEEE Computer Society, New York, December 1984, 24 pp.

Morgan, Hal and Dan Symmes, *Amazing 3-D,* Little, Brown, and Co., Boston, 1983.

Piaget, Jean and Bärbel Inhelder, *The Child's Conception of Space,* W.W. Norton and Company, New York, 1967, 490 pp.

Pevsner, Nikolaus, *An Outline of European Architecture,* Penguin Books, Baltimore, 1963, 496 pp.

Stevens, Peter S., *Handbook of Regular Patterns: An Introduction to Symmetry in Two Dimensions,* MIT Press, Cambridge, 1981, 400 pp.

Thomas, Richard K., *Three-Dimensional Design: A cellular Approach,* Van Nostrand Reinhold, New York, 1969, 96 pp.

Thompson, D'Arcy, *On Growth and Form,* ed. J.T. Bonner, Cambridge University Press, Cambridge, 1966, 346 pp.

Weyle, Hermann, *Symmetry,* Princeton University Press, Princeton, 1966, 168 pp.

1.3 An Annotated for Graphic Design of Spatial Displays

Berkman, Aaron, *Art and Space*, Social Sciences Publishers, New York, 1949, 175 pp.

Bertin, Jacques, *Semiology of Graphics*, trans. W.J. Berg, The University of Wisconsin Press, Madison, 1983, ISBN 0-299-09060-4, 415 pp.

Bolt, Richard A., *The Human Interface: Where People and Computers Meet*, Lifetime Learning Publications, Wadsworth International, Belmont, CA, 1989, ISBN 0-534-03380-6, 113 pp.

Critchlow, Keith, *Order in Space*: *A Design Source Book*, Studio Book, Viking Press, New York, 1970, ISBN 670-52830-7, 120 pp.

Ellis, Stephen R., ed., *Proceedings,* Spatial Displays and Spatial Instruments Conference, NASA Conference Publication, 1989.

Ghyka, Matila, *The Geometry of Art and Life*, Sheed and Ward, New York, 1946, 174 pp.

Gould, Laura, and William Finzer, *Programming by Rehearsal*, Tech. report SCL-84-1, Xerox Palo Alto Research Center, May 1984, 133 pp.

Gregory, Richard L., *The Intelligent Eye*, McGraw-Hill, New York, 1970, LC-72-97117, 191 pp.

——, *Eye and Brain*: *The Psychology of Seeing*, World University Library, McGraw-Hill, New York, 1968, LC 64-66178, 251 pp.

Hall, Edward T., *The Hidden Dimension*, Anchor Books, New York, 1982, ISBN 0-385-08476-5, 217 pp.

——, *The Silent Language*, Fawcett World Library, New York, 1963, 192 pp.

Hambidge, Jay, *The Elements of Dynamic Symmetry,* Dover Publications, New York, 1967, LC 66-30210, 113 pp.

Herdeg, Walter, ed., *Graphis Diagrams*, Graphis Press, Zurich, 1981, ISBN 3-85709-410-9, 205 pp.

Ivins, William M., Jr., *Art and Geometry: A Study in Space Intuitions*, Dover Publications, New York, 1946, LC 64-156511, 113 pp.

Jencks, Charles, and William Chaitkin, *Architecture Today*, Harry N. Abrams, New York, 1982, ISBN 0-8109-0669-04, 359 pp.

Lakoff, George, and Mark Johnson, *Metaphors We Live By*, The University of Chicago Press, Chicago, 1984, ISBN 0-226-46800-3, 242 pp.

Lockwood, Arthur, *Diagrams*, Watson-Guptill Publications, New York, 1969, British ISBN 289-37030-2, 144 pp.

Loran, Erle, *Cézanne's Composition: Analysis of His Form with Diagrams and Photographs of His Motifs*, University of California Press, Berkeley, 1963, 143 pp.

March, Lionel, and Philip Steadman, *The Geometry of Environment: An Introduction to Spatial Organization in Design*, RIBA Publications, London, 1971, 360 pp.

Marcus, Aaron "Corporate Identity for Iconic Interface Design: The Graphic Design Perspective," *IEEE Computer Graphics and Applications* 4, no. 7, December 1984, pp. 24ff.

——, et al.,"Screen Design Guidelines," *Proceedings National Computer Graphics Association Annual Conference and Exposition,* 14-18 April 1985, National Computer Graphics Association, Fairfax, VA, 1985, pp. 105-137.

Morgan, Hal, and Dan Symmes, *Amazing 3-D*, Little, Brown, and Co., Boston, 1983 ISBN 0-316-58283-2, 176 pp.

Piaget, Jean, and Bärbel Inhelder, *The Child's Conception of Space*, W.W. Norton and Co., New York, 1967, ISBN 393-00408-2, 490 pp.

Pevsner, Nikolaus, *An Outline of European Architecture*, Penguin Books, Baltimore, 1963, 496 pp.

Stevens, Peter S., *Handbook of Regular Patters: An Introduction to Symmetry in Two Dimensions*, MIT Press, Cambridge, 1981, ISBN 0-262-19188-1, 400 pp.

Thomas, Richard K., *Three-Dimensional Design: A Cellular Approach*, Van Nostrand Reinhold Co., New York, 1969, ISBN 0-442-313488-9, 96 pp.

Thompson, D'Arcy, *On Growth and Form*, ed. J.T. Bonner, Cambridge University Press, Cambridge, 1966, 346 pp.

Weyl, Hermann, *Symmetry*, Princeton University Press, Princeton, 1966, 168 pp.

2.1 Making Type Decisions

Bigelow, Charles, and Donald Day, "Digital Typography," *Scientific American*, 250, no. 2, August 1983, pp. 106-119.

Craig, James, *Production for the Graphic Designer,* Watson-Guptil Publications, New York, 1974.

Gerstner, Carl, *Compendium for Literates: A System of Writing,* MIT Press, Cambridge, 1974.

Haley, Allan, *Phototypography*, Charles Scribner's Sons, New York, 1980.

Hartley, James, *Designing Instructional Text*, Nichols Publishing Co., New York, 1978.

Laundy, Peter, and Massimo Vignelli, *"Graphic Design for Non-Profit Organizations,"* American Institute of Graphic Arts, New York, 1980.

Marcus, Aaron, "Corporate Identity for Iconic Interface Design: The Graphic Design Perspective," *Proc.,* Vol. 2, National Computer Graphics Association, Fairfax, VA, 1984, pp. 468-479.

——"Designing the Face of an Interface," *IEEE Computer Graphics and Applications* 2, no. 1, January 1982, pp. 23-30.

——Managing Facts and Concepts, National Endowment for the Arts, Design Arts Program, Washington, D.C., 1983.

Mueller-Brockmann, Josef, *Grid Systems in Graphic Design*, Verlag Arthur Niggli, Niederteufen, Switzerland, 1981.

Rehe, Rolf F., *Typography: How to Make It Most Legible*, Design Research International, Carmel, IN, 1974.

Ruder, Emil, *Typography: A Manual of Design,* Verlag Arthur Niggli, Niederteufen, Switzerland, 1977.

Trollip, Stanley R., and Gregory Sales, "Readability of Computer-Generated Fill-Justified Text," *Human Factors* 28, No. 2, 1986, 159-163.

Vignelli, Massimo, "Grids: Their Meaning and Use for Federal Designers," no. 036-000-00038-4, National Endowment for the Arts, Design Arts Program, Washington, D.C., 1976

2.2 Forms Design

Burgess, John H., *Human Factors in Forms Design*, Nelson-Hall, ISBN 0-88229-539-X, Chicago, 1984.

Duffy, Thomas M., and R. Waller, eds., *Designing Usable Texts*, Academic Press, Orlando, FL, 1985, ISBN 0-12-223260-7.

Felker, Daniel B., et al., *Guidelines for Document Designers*, American Institute for Research, Washington, D.C., 1981.

Fleming, Malcolm, and W. Howard Levie, Instructional Message Design: Principles from the *Behavioral Sciences,* Educational Technology Publication, Englewood Cliffs, NJ, 1978, ISBN 0-87778-104-4.

Hartley, James, *Designing Instructional Text*, Nichols Publishing Co., New York, 1978, ISBN 0-89397-034-4.

Jonassen, David H., ed. *The Technology of Text,* Educational Technology Publications, Englewood Cliffs, NJ, 1982, ISBN 00-87778-182-6.

Mueller-Brockman, Josef, *Grid Systems in Graphic Design*, Verlag Arthur Niggli, Niederteufen, Switzerland, 1981.

Raines, Gar, ed. *Forms for the '80's: How to Design and Produce Them*, North American Publishing Co., Philadelphia, 1981, ISBN 0-912920-54-8.

White, Jan V., *Editing by Design*, 2d ed., R. R. Bowker Company, New York, 1982.

——*Using Charts and Graphs*, R. R. Bowker Co., New York, 1984, ISBN 08352-1894-5.

2.3 The Typography of Complex Documentation: Computer Programs

Apollinaire, Guillaume, *Calligrammes*; *Poems of Peace and War 1913-1916*, University of California Press, London, 1980.

Baecker, Ron, and Aaron Marcus, "Design Principles for the Enhanced Presentation of Computer Program Source Text," *Proc., Conference on Human Factors in Computing Systems* (SIGCHI '86), Boston, April 1986, pp. 51-58.

———, *Human Factors and Typography for More Readable Programs*, Addison-Wesley Publishing Co, Reading, MA, 1990.

———, "On Enhancing the Interface to the Source Code of Computer Programs," *Proc., Human Factors in Computing Systems* (SIGCHI '83), Boston, December 1983, pp. 251-255.

Baecker, Ron, et al.,"Enhancing the Presentation of Computer Program Source Text," Final 6 vol. report of the Program Visualization Project, DARPA, submitted by Human Computing Resources Corp., Toronto, Ontario and Aaron Marcus and Associates, Emeryville, CA, 1985.

Kernighan, Brian, and Donald Ritchie, *The C Programming Language,* Prentice-Hall, Inc. Englewood Cliffs, NJ, 1978.

Marcus, Aaron, and Ron Baecker, "On the Graphic Design of Program Text," *Proc., Graphics Interface '82*, Toronto, 1982, 302-311.

Wendt, Dirk, "An Experimental Approach to the Improvement of the Typographic Design of Textbooks," *Visible Language* 13, no. 2, 1979, pp. 108-133.

3.1 Clarity and Consistency in Icon Design

Aicher, Otl, and Martin Krampen, *Zeichensysteme der Visuellen Kommunikation* (Sign Systems of Visual Communication), Alexander Koch Publishers, Stuttgart, 1977.

American Institute of Graphic Arts, *Symbol Signs*, Visual Communication Books, Hastings House, New York, 1981.

Bliss, C. K., *Semantography,* Semantography (Blissymbolics) Publications, Sydney, Australia, 1965.

Diethelm, Walter, with M. Diethelm, *Signet, Signal, Symbol*, ABC Verlag, Zurich, 1970.

Dreyfuss, Henry, *Symbol Sourcebook*, McGraw-Hill, New York, 1972.

Green, Paul, and William T. Burgess, "Debugging a Symbol Set for Identifying Displays: Production and Screening Studies," no. PB81-113573, U.S. Department of Commerce, National Technical Information Service, Springfield, VA, Prepared by the Highway Safety Research Institute, Tech. report UM-HSRI-80-64, The University of Michigan, September 1980.

Loddings, Ken, "Iconic Interfacing," *Computer Graphics and Applications 3*, no. 2, March-April 1983, pp. 11-20.

Marcus, Aaron, *"Corporate Identity for Iconic Interface Design: The Graphic Design Perspective,"* *Proc.,* Vol. 2, National Computer Graphics Association, Fairfax, VA, 1984, pp. 468-479.

——, *Managing Facts and Concepts*, National Endowment for the Arts, Design Arts Program, Washington, D.C., 1983.

Markowitz, J., et al., "An Investigation of the Design and Performance of Traffic Control Devices," no. PB 182 534, U.S. Department of Commerce, National Technical Information Service, Springfield, VA, 1968.

Neurath, Otto, International Picture Language, facsimile reprint, University of Reading, England, 1980.

Ota, Yukio, "LoCoS: an Experimental Pictorial Language," *Icographic,* no. 6, 1973, pp. 15-19.

Ruder, Emil, *Type, Sign Symbol,* ABC Verlag, Zurich, 1980.

3.2 Icon Design Tips

American Institute of Graphic Arts, *Symbol Signs,* Visual Communication Books, Hastings House, New York, ISBN 0-8038-6777-8.

Dreyfuss, Henry, *Symbol Sourcebook*, McGraw-Hill, New York, 1972.

Green, Paul, and William T. Burgess, "Debugging a Symbol Set for Identifying Displays: Production and Screening Studies," no. P81-113573, U.S. Department of Commerce, National Technical Information Service, Springfield, VA. Prepared by Highway Safety Research Institute, Tech. report UM-HSRI-80-64, The University of Michigan, September 1980.

Kluth, Daniel J., and Steven W. Lundberg, "Design Patents: A New Form of Intellectual Property Protection for Computer Software," *The Computer Lawyer* 5, no. 8, August 1988, pp. 1-10.

Ota, Yukio, *Pictogram Design*, Kashiwashobo, Tokyo, 1987, ISBN 4-7601-0300-7-C2070. USA orders: Books Nippon, 115 West 57 Street, New York, NY 10019, 212-582-4622. Note: One of the most recent, complete, and useful documents available for icon designers. The Ota book *Pictogram Design* together with the classic Dreyfuss *Symbol Sourcebook* and The American Institute of Graphic Arts *Symbol Signs*, which are listed in this Bibliography, constitute an essential library for designing state-of-the-art icons and symbols.

3.3 Icon Design in a CAD/CAM Graphical User Interface: A Case Study

Computervision, "The CADD Station System," Computervision Corporation, Bedford, MA, September 1986.

Marcus, Aaron, "CAD/CAM from the Graphic Design Perspective," *Proc. Second Symposium on Automation Technology in Engineering Data Handling and CAD/CAM*, Automation Technology Institute, Monterey, CA 1982. (Also published as Lawrence Berkeley Laboratory tech. report LBL-15578, November 1982.)

——"CAE/CAM Tablet Design: A Case Study," *Proc., Seventh Symposium on Automation Technology in Engineering Data Handling and CAD/CAM*, Automation Technology Institute, Monterey, California, 1986, 10 pages unnumbered.

——"Corporate Identity for Iconic Interface Design: The Graphic Design Perspective," *IEEE Computer Graphics and Applications 4*, no. 12, December 1984, pp. 24-32.

Whitney, R. Lee, "CAD Productivity and the User Interface," *Computer Graphics World 9*, no. 10, October 1986, pp. 85-86.

3.4 An Annotated Bibliography of Signs, Icons, and Symbols

Aicher, Otto, and Martin Krampen, *Zeichensysteme der Visuellen Kommunikation* (Sign Systems of Visual Communication), Alexander Koch Publishers, Stuttgart, 1977, ISBN 3-87422-565-8, 154 pp.

American Institute of Graphic Arts, *Symbol Signs*, Visual Communication Books, Hastings House, New York 1981, ISBN 0-8038-6777-8, 240 pp.

Arnstein, J., *The International Dictionary of Graphic Symbols,* Kogan Page Ltd., Whitstable, Kent, England, 1983, ISBN 0-85038-578-4, 239 pp.

Bliss, C.K., *Semantography,* Semantography (Blissymbolics) Publications, Sydney, Australia, 1965, 882 pp.

Cirlot, J.E., *A Dictionary of Symbols,* trans. J. Sage, Philosophical Library, New York, 1962, 400 pp.

Diethelm, Walter, with M. Diethelm, *Signet, Signal, Symbol,* ABC Verlag, Zurich, 1970, 226 pp.

Dreyfuss, Henry, *Symbol Sourcebook,* McGraw-Hill, New York, 1972, ISBN 07-017837-2, 292 pp.

Green, Paul, and W.T. Burgess, "Debugging a Symbol Set for Identifying Displays: Production and Screening Studies," Tech. report UM-HSRI-80-64, Highway Safety Research Institute, NTIS, no. PB81-113573, September 1980, 116 pp.

Jung, Carl G., *Man and his Symbols,* Doubleday and Co., Garden City, NY, 1964, ISBN 0-385-05221-9, 320 pp.

Kuyayama, Y., *Trademarks & Symbols,* 2 vols., Van Nostrand Reinhold Co., New York, 1973. Vol. 1: ISBN 0-442-24563-7, 193 pp.; Vol. 2: ISBN 0-442-24563-7, 186 pp.

Lerner, N.D., and B.L. Collins, "The Assessment of Safety Symbol Understandability by Different Testing Methods," U.S. Department of Commerce, Natural Bureau of Standards, Environmental Design Research Division, August 1980, 51 pp.

Modley, Rudolf, with William R. Myers, *Handbook of Pictorial Symbols,* Dover Publications, New York, 1976, ISBN 0-486-23357-X, 143 pp.

Neurath, O., *International Picture Language,*
University of Reading, England, 1980, 70 pp.

Ota, Y., "LoCoS: An Experimental Pictorial
Language," *Icographic*, International Council of
Graphic Design Associations (ICOGRADA), POB 398,
London W11-4UG, England. no. 6, 1973, pp. 15-19.

Shepherd, W., *Shepherd's Glossary of Graphic Signs
and Symbols,* Dover Publications, New York, 1971,
ISBN 0-486-20700-5, 587 pp.

"Signs and Display Systems, Graphic Design, and
Human Engineering, PB82-808585, U.S. Department
of Commerce, National Technical Information Service,
June 1982, 170 pp.

Smeets, R., *Signs, Symbols & Ornaments,* Van
Nostrand Reinhold Co., New York, 1982, ISBN
0-442-27800-4, 176 pp.

Weilgart, J.W., *AUI: The Language of Space,* 1974,
341 pp. and *Cosmic Elements of Meaning: Symbols of
the Spirit's Life,* Cosmic Communication Co., Decorah,
IA. 1975, 303 pp.

4.1 The Ten Commandments of Color

Albers, Josef, *Interaction of Color*, Yale University
Press, New Haven, 1975.

Berlin, Brent, and P. Kay, *Basic Color Terms*,
University of California Press, Berkeley, 1969.

Birren, Faber, *Color and Human Response*, Van
Nostrand Reinhold Co., New York, 1978.

——*Color Psychology and Color Therapy*, The Citadel
Press, Secaucus, NJ, 1961.

—— ed., *Munsell: A Grammar of Color,* Van Nostrand
Reinhold Co., New York, 1969.

Durett, John, and Judi Trezona, "How to Use Color Displays Effectively," *Byte* 7, no. 4, April 1982, pp. 50-53.

Fromme, Francine, "Incorporating the Human Factor in Color CAD Systems," *IEEE Proceedings of the 20th Design Automation Conference,* 1983, pp. 189-195.

Jones, Gerald E., "Color Use, Abuse in Presentations," *Computer Graphics World* 9, no. 5, May 1986, pp. 119-120ff.

Kelly, Kenneth L., "The Universal Color Language," in Kelly, Kenneth L., and D. B. Judd, *Color: Universal Language and Dictionary of Names*, no. 003-003-017-051, U.S. Department of Commerce, National Bureau of Standards, December, 1976.

Kuehni, Rolf G., *Color: Essence and Logic*, Van Nostrand Reinhold Co., New York, 1983.

Kueppers, Harald, *The Basic Law of Color Theory,* Barron Educational Series, Inc., Woodbury, NY, 1980.

——*Color: Origin, Systems, Uses,* trans. F. Bradley, Van Nostrand Reinhold Co., New York, 1972.

Lamberski, Richard J., "A Comprehensive and Critical Review of the Methodology and Findings in Color Investigations," *Proc., Conference of the Association for Educational Communications and Technology*, Association for Educational Communications and Technology, Denver, CO, April 1980, (ERIC IR008916/ED194063).

Marcus, Aaron, "Color: A Tool for Computer Graphics Communication," in Greenberg, Don, et al., *The Computer Image*: *Applications of Computer Graphics*, Addison-Wesley Publishing Co., Reading, MA, 1982, pp. 76-90.

——"Users Must Establish Own Rules for Color," *Computer Graphics Today* 2, no. 9, September 1985, pp. 7ff.

Merry, Madeline, "Color for Computers Demands Special Care," *ID Magazine* 29, no. 4, November-December 1982, pp. 15-16.

Murch, Gerald M., "Effective Use of Color: Cognitive Principles," *Tekniques* 8, Summer 1984, pp. 25-31.

——"Physiological Principles for the Effective Use of Color," *IEEE Computer Graphics and Applications* 4, no. 11, November 1984, pp. 49-54.

Stockton, James, *Designer's Guide to Color*, Vols. 1 and 2, Chronicle Books, San Francisco, 1984.

Taylor, Joann M., and Gerald M. Murch, "The Effective Use of Color in Visual Displays: Text and Graphics Applications," *Color Research and Application* 11, Supplement 1986, pp. S3-S10.

Thorell, Lisa G., and Wanda J. Smith, *Using Computer Color Effectively,* Prentice Hall, Inc., Englewood Cliffs, NJ, 1990.

Varley, Helen, *Colour*, Marshall Editions, Ltd., London, 1983.

4.2 An Annotated Bibliography of Color

Albers, Josef, *Interaction of Color*, Yale University Press, New Haven, 1975, 81 pp.

Barker, E., and M. J. Krebs, *Color Coding Effects on Human Performance, An Annotated Bibliography,* U.S. Office of Naval Research, Arlington, VA, April 1977, 91 pp.

Berlin, B., and P. Kay, *Basic Color Terms,* University of California Press, Berkeley, 1969, 178 pp.

Birren, Faber, *Color and Human Response,* Van Nostrand Reinhold Co., New York, 1978, 0-442-20787-5, 141 pp.

——*Principles of Color,* Van Nostrand Reinhold Co., New York, 1969, ISBN 0-442-20774-3, 96 pp.

Chevreul, M.E., *The Principles of Harmony and Contrast of Colors and Their Applications to the Arts,* Van Nostrand Reinhold Co, New York, 1981, ISBN 0-442-2121207, 224 pp.

Chijiwa, H., *Color Harmony,* Rockport Publishers, Rockport, MA, 1987, ISBN 0-935603-06-9, 158 pp.

"Consumer Color Charts, Munsell Color," Kollmorgen Corp., Macbeth Division, Baltimore, 16 pp.

Cowan, William B., *Color Research and Application,* special ed., Vol. 11, 1986, 92 pp.

de Grandis, Luigina, *Theory and Use of Color,* trans. A. Mondadori, Harry N. Abrams, New York, 1984, ISBN 0-8109-2317-3, 159 pp.

Itten, Josef, *The Art of Color,* Van Nostrand Reinhold Co., New York, 1973, ISBN 0-422-24037-6, 155 pp.

——*The Elements of Color,* Van Nostrand Reinhold Co., New York, 1970, ISBN 0-442-24038-4, 95 pp.

Kelly, K.L., and D.B. Judd, *Color: Universal Language and Dictionary of Names,* U.S. Department of Commerce, National Bureau of Standards, December 1976, 158 pp. no. 003-003-01705-1.

Kobayashi, S., with R. Sternberg, *A Book of Colors,* Kodansha International, Harper Row, New York, 1987, ISBN 0-87011-800-5, 128 pp.

Kuehni, R.G., *Color: Essence and Logic,* Van Nostrand Reinhold Co., New York, 1983, 138 pp.

Kueppers, H., *Color Atlas,* Barron's Educational Series, Inc. Woodbury, NY, 1982, ISBN 0-8120-2172-X, 170 pp.

——*Color: Origin, Systems, Users,* trans. F. Bradley, Van Nostrand Reinhold Co., New York, 1972, ISBN 0-442-29985-0, 155 pp,

Lamberski, Richard J., "A Comprehensive and Critical Review of the Methodology and Findings in Color Investigations," *Proc. Annual Convention of the Association of Educational Communications and Technology,* no. ED-194063/IR008916, Association for Educational Communications & Technology, Denver, CO, April 1980, 338-379, pp.

Marx, E., *Optical Color and Simultaneity,* trans. Geoffrey O'Brien, Van Nostrand Reinhold Co., New York, 1983, ISBN 0-442-23864-9, 152 pp.

Munsell, A.H., *A Grammar of Color, ed.* F. Birren, Van Nostrand Reinhold Co., New York, 1969, LC 69-15896, 96 pp.

Ostwald, William, *The Color Primer,* ed. F. Birren, Van Nostrand Reinhold Co., New York, 1969, LC 69-15897, 96 pp.

"Pantone Color Guide," Pantone, Inc., Moonachie, NJ.

"Process Color Guide," 2d ed., S.D. Scott Printing Co., New York, 1986, 96 pp.

Rossotti, H., *Colour,* Princeton University Press, Princeton, 1983, ISBN 0-691-02386-7, 239 pp.

Rowell, J., *Picture Perfect: Color Output for Computer Graphics,* Tecktronix Inc., Beaverton, OR, 1990, Part No. 070-6559-00.

Sloane, P., *Color: Basic Principles and New Directions,* Reinhold Studio Vista, London, 1968.

Southworth, M., *Pocket Guide to Color Reproduction: Communication and Control*, Graphic Arts Publishing Co., Livonia, NY, 1979, ISBN 0-933600-01-1, 106 pp.

Thorell, Lisa G., and Wanda J. Smith, *Using Computer Color Effectively,* Prentice Hall, Inc., Englewood Cliffs, NJ, 1990.

5.1 Chart Design

Carlsen, Robert D., and Donald L. Vest, *Encyclopedia of Business Charts*, Prentice-Hall, Inc., Englewood Cliffs, NJ, 1977.

Chambers, John M., et al., *Graphical Methods for Data Analysis*, Wadsworth International Group, Belmont, CA, 1983.

Huff, Darell, *How to Lie with Statistics,* W. W. Norton and Co., New York, 1951.

Jarett, Irwin M., *Computer Graphics and Reporting Financial Data,* John Wiley and Sons, New York, 1983.

MacGregor, A. J., *Graphics Simplified*, University of Toronto Press, Toronto, 1979.

Marcus, Aaron, "Computer-Assisted Chartmaking from the Graphic Design Perspective," *Computer Graphics, Proc., ACM SIGGRAPH Conference,* no. 3, Association for Computing Machinery, New York, July 1980, pp. 247-253.

——"Managing Facts and Concepts," National Endowment for the Arts, Design Arts Program, Washington, D.C., 1983.

Matkowski, Betty S., "Steps to Effective Business Graphics," Hewlett-Packard Co., San Diego, CA, 1983.

Meyers, Cecil H., *Handbook of Basic Graphs: A Modern Approach*, Wadsworth Publishing Co., Belmont, CA, 1970 (out of print).

Paller, Alan, Kethryn Szoka, and Nan Nelson, "Choosing the Right Chart," Integrated Software Systems Corp., San Diego, 1981.

Schmid, Calvin F., and Stanton E. Schmid, *Handbook of Graphic Presentation,* 2d ed., John Wiley and Sons, New York, 1979.

Spear, Mary Eleanor, *Practical Charting Techniques*, McGraw-Hill, New York, 1969.

Tufte, Edward R., *Envisioning Information*, Graphics Press, Cheshire, CT, 1990.

——*The Visual Display of Quantitative Information*, Graphics Press, Cheshire, CT, 1983.

5.2 An Annotated Bibliography of Chart and Diagram Design

Auger, B.Y., *How to Run Better Business Meetings*, 3M Company, St. Paul., 1979, 214 pp.

Bertin, Jacques, *Semiology of Graphics,* trans. William J. Berg, The University of Wisconsin Press, Madison, 1983, 415 pp.

Carlsen, Robert D., and Donald L. Vest, *Encyclopedia of Business Charts,* Prentice-Hall, Inc., Englewood Cliffs, NJ, 1977, 886 pp.

Chambers, John, M., et al., *Graphical Methods for Data Analysis,* Wadsworth Statistics/Probability Series, Wadsworth International Group, Belmont, CA, 1983, 395 pp.

The Diagram Group, *Visual Comparisons,* St. Martin's Press, New York, 1980, 240 pp.

Heller, Steven, and Philip B. Meggs, *Graphic Design USA: 7,* The Annual of the American Institute of Graphic Arts, Watson-Guptil Publications, New York, 1986, pp. 248-319.

Herdeg, Walter, ed., *Graphis Diagrams,* Graphis Press, Zurich, 1981, 207 pp.

Holmes, Nigel, *Designer's Guide to Creating Charts and Diagrams,* Watson-Guptill Publications, 1984, 192 pp.

Huff, Darrell, *How to Lie with Statistics,* W.W. Norton and Co., New York, 1951, 142 pp.

Japan Creators' Association, ed., *Diagraphics,* Japan Creators' Association Press, Tokyo, 1986, 304 pp.

Lockwood, Arthur, *Diagrams,* Watson-Guptill Publications, New York, 1969 (out of print), 144 pp.

MacGregor, A.J., *Graphics Simplified,* University of Toronto Press, Toronto, 1979, 64 pp.

Martin, James, and Carma McClure, *Diagramming Techniques for Analysts and Programmers,* Prentice-Hall, Inc., Englewood Cliffs, NJ, 1985, 396 pp.

Meilach, Donna Z., *Dynamics of Presentation Graphics,* Dow Jones-Irwin, Homewood, IL, 1986, 259 pp.

Meyers, Cecil H., *Handbook of Basic Graphs: A Modern Approach,* Wadsworth International Group, Belmont, CA, 1970 (out of print), 214 pp.

Schmid, Calvin F., and Standon E. Schmid, *Handbook of Graphic Presentation,* 2d ed., John Wiley and Sons, New York, 1979, 308 pp.

Tufte, Edward R., *Envisioning Information,* Graphics Press, Cheshire, CT, 1990, 200 pp.

—— *The Visual Display of Quantitative Information,* Graphics Press, Cheshire, CT, 1983, 197 pp.

Tukey, John, W., *Exploratory Data Analysis,* Addison-Wesley Publishing Co., Inc., Reading, MA, 1977, 688 pp.

White, Jan V., *Using Charts and Graphs,* R. R. Bowker Co., New York, 1984, 202 pp.

5.3 An Annotated Bibliography of Map Design

Albers, Josef, Interaction of Color, Yale University Press, New Haven, 1975, 81 pp.

Anderson, Robert, Robert Helms, and Norman Z. Shapiro, "Design Considerations for Computer-Based Interactive Map Display Systems," report no. R-2382-ARPA, prepared for DARPA by the Rand Corporation, Santa Monica, CA, February 1979, 45 pp.

Artscanada, no. 188/189 Spring 1974, 106 pp.

Bertin, Jacques, *Semiology of Graphics*, trans. William J. Berg, The University of Wisconsin Press, Madison, 1983, ISBN 0-299-09060-4, 415 pp.

Brown, Lloyd A., *The Story of Maps*, Dover Publications, New York, 1977, ISBN 0-486-23873-3, 397 pp.

Gould, Peter, and Rodney White, *Mental Maps*, Penguin Books, Baltimore, 1974, 204 pp.

Guelke, Leonard, ed., "The Nature of Cartographic Communication," Monograph no. 19, Supplement no. 1 to *Canadian Cartographer* 14, 1977, 147 pp, published by B.V. Gutsell, Department of Geography, York University, Toronto.

Harvey, P.D.A., *The History of Topographical Maps*, Thames and Hudson, 1980, LC 80-80086, 199 pp.

Herdeg, Walter, ed., *Graphis Diagrams*, Graphis Press, Zurich, 1981, ISBN 3-85709-410-9, 207 pp.

Hooper, Kristina, "Experiential Mapping," no. R-3478-ARPA, DARPA, Arlington, VA, 1981, 276 pp.

Lockwood, Arthur, *Diagrams*, Watson-Guptill Publications, New York, 1969, British ISBN 289-37030-2, 144 pp.

"Map Data Catalog," U.S. Department of the Interior, National Cartographic Information Center National Mapping Program, Washington.

"Maps of the World's Nations," Vol 1: Western Hemisphere, no. 041-00078-1, Central Intelligence Agency, Washington, January 1976, 46 pp.

Muehrcke, Philip, "Thematic Cartography," Resource paper no. 19, Assoc. of American Geographers, Washington, 1972, LC 72-77214, 66 pp.

"Process Color Guide," 2d ed., S.D. Scott Printing Co., New York, 1986, 96 pp.

Peucker, Thomas K. "Computer Cartography," Resource paper no. 17, Assoc. of American Geographers, Washington, 1972, LC 72-75261, 75 pp.

Robinson, Arthur H., and Barbara Bartz Petchenik, *The Nature of Maps*, University of Chicago Press, Chicago, 1976, ISBN 0-226-72281-3, 138 pp.

Robinson Arthur, Randall Sale, and Joel Morrison, *Elements of Cartography*, John Wiley and Sons, New York, 1978, ISBN 0-471-01781-7, 448 pp.

Weltman, Gershon, "Maps: A Guide to Innovative Design," Report no. PTR-1033S-78-1, prepared for DARPA by Perceptronics, Woodland Hills, CA, February 1979, 249 pp.

6.1 Common User-Interface Design

Marcus, Aaron, "Corporate Identity for Iconic Interface Design: The Graphic Design Perspective," *IEEE Computer Graphics and Application* 4 no. 7, December 1984, pp. 24ff.

——"Graphic Design for Computer Graphics," *IEEE Computer Graphics and Applications* 2, no. 7, July 1983, pp. 63-82.

Rosenberg, Daniel, "Internal vs. External Metaphor in the Design of a 'Smart' Product User Interface," *Proc., Interface '87*, Human Factors Society, Santa Monica, CA, 1987, pp. 149-156.

——"Corporate User Interface Standards: A New Component of Product Form," *Innovation*, Spring, 1988.

Rosenberg, Daniel, and Aaron Marcus, "Common User Interface Design: The Kodak Approach," no. A8D027, Eastman Kodak Company, Rochester, NY, May 1988.

6.2 The User-Interface Standards Manual

Baecker, Ron, and Aaron Marcus, *Human Factors and Typography for More Readable Programs*, Addison-Wesley Publishing Co., Reading, MA, 1990.

Brown, C. Marlin, *Human-Computer Interface Design Guidelines*, Ablex Publishing, Norwood, NJ, 1986.

Eco, Umberto, *A Theory of Semiotics*, Indiana University Press, Bloomington, 1976.

Marcus, Aaron, "Bibliography of Graphic Design for Computer Graphics," *Proc.*, Vol. 1, National Computer Graphics Association, Fairfax, VA 1984, pp. 253-260.

——, "A Case Study of Seedis," *The Design Journal* 1, no. 1, 1984, pp. 17ff.

——"Corporate Identity for Iconic Interface Design: The Graphic Design Perspective," *IEEE Computer Graphics and Applications 4,* no. 12, December 1984, pp. 24ff.

——"Designing the Face of an Interface," *IEEE Computer Graphics and Applications* 12, no. 1, January 1982, pp. 23-29.

——"A Prototype Computerized Page-Design System," *Visible Language* 5, no. 3, Summer 1971, pp. 197-220.

——"User Interface Manuals Guide Developers," *Computer Graphics Today* 2, no. 7, July 1985, pp. 7ff.

Marcus, A. et al., "Screen Design Guidelines" *Proc., National Computer Graphics Association Annual Conference*, Fairfax, VA, 1985, pp. 105-135.

Marcus, A., et al., "A Visible Language Program for Perq's Accent Operating System," *Proc., National Computer Graphics Association*, Fairfax, VA, 1985, pp. 481-490.

McCormick, Kathleen A., and Teresa Bleser, "Developing a User Interface Styleguide," *Proc.,* National Computer Graphics Association, Fairfax, VA, 1985, pp. 518-527.

7 A Comparison of Graphical User Interfaces

American National Standards Institute, "X Window System Data Stream Definition," Working Draft, New York, June 1988.

Apple Computer, *Human Interface Guidelines: The Apple Desktop Interface*, Addison-Wesley Publishing Co., Reading, MA, 1989.

Bannon, L., et al., "Evaluation and Analysis of Users Activity Organization," *Proceedings of the CHI '83 Human Factors in Computing Systems Conference,* ACM, New York, pp. 54-57.

Billingsley, P.A. "Taking Panes: Issues in the Design of Windowing Systems," in Helander, M., ed., *Handbook of Human-Computer Interaction,* Elsevier Science Publishers, Eindhoven, Netherlands pp. 413-436.

Bly, Sarah A., and Jarret K. Rosenberg, "A Comparison of Tiled and Overlapping Windows," Proceedings of the CHI '86 Human Factors in *Computing Systems Conference,* ACM, New York, pp. 101-106.

Bury, K.F., Davies, S.E., and M.J. Darnell, *Window Management: A Review of Issues and Some Results from User Testing,* IBM report HFC-53, IBM Human Factors Center, San Jose, 1985.

Card, Stuart K., "Windows: Why They were Invented, How They Help," *The Office,* March 1985, pp. 52-54.

Card, Stuart K., and Austin Henderson, "A Multiple, Virtual-Workspace Interface to Support User Task Switching," *Proceedings of the CHI '87 Human Factors in Computing Systems Conference,* ACM, New York, pp. 53-59.

Card, Stuart K., Pavel, M., and J.E. Farrell, "Window-Based Computer Dialogues," in *Human Computer Interaction-Interact '84,* Amsterdam, Netherlands, 1984 pp. 239-243.

Champlin, V.L., "Unix Application Network Interfaces," *UniForum 1989 Conference Proceedings,* UniForum, Mountain View, CA, 1988, pp. 147-154.

Christeson, B., Horrell, S., and J. Oldroyd, "Comparison of User Interfaces," The Instruction Set, Ltd., London, 1989.

Davies, S.E., Bury, K.F., and M.J. Darnell, "An Experimental Comparison of a Windowed vs. a Non-Windowed Operating System Environment," *Proceedings of the Human Factors Society 29th Annual Meeting,* The Human Factors Society, Santa Monica, 1985, pp. 250-254.

Dunwoody, J.C., and M.A. Linton, "A Dynamic Profile of Window System Usage," *Proceedings of the 2nd IEEE Conference on Computer Workstations,* Santa Clara, CA, 1988, pp. 90-99.

Farrell, J., and D.A. LavaLee, "User Interfaces in Window Systems: Architecture and Implementation," *CHI '89 Tutorial Course Note"* no. 25, ACM/SIGCHI, ACM, New York, 1989.

Gaylin, K.B., "How are Windows Used? Some Notes on Creating an Empirically Based Windowing Benchmark Test," *Proceedings of the CHI '86 Human Factors in Computing Systems Conference,* ACM, New York, pp. 96-100.

Grossman, M.S., and G.E. Williams, "Real-Time Resource Sharing for Graphics Workstations, Proceedings of the Usenix Association Winter *Conference,* Usenix, Berkeley, CA, 1986, pp. 24-33.

Hayes, F., and N. Baran, "A Guide to GUI's," *Byte* 14, no. 7, July 1989, pp. 250-257.

Henderson, Austin, and Stuart K. Card, "Rooms: the Use of Multiple Virtual Workspaces to Reduce Space Contention in a Window-Based Graphical Interface," *ACM Transactions on Graphics* 5, no. 3, pp. 211-243.

Hoeber, T. "The OPEN LOOK Graphical User Interface," *UniForum 1989 Conference Proceedings,* UniForum, Mountain View, CA, 1989, pp. 29-47.

Jacobs, T.W.R., "The XView Toolkit: An Architectural Overview," in Farrell, J., and D. A. LavaLee, "User Interfaces as Window Systems: Architecture and Implementation," *CHI '89 Tutorial Course Notes no. 25*, ACM/SIGCHI, ACM, New York, 1989, pp. 95-114.

Johnson-Laird, A., "They Look Good in Demos, But Windows are a Real Pain," *Software News,* April 1985, pp. 36-37.

Jones, J.M., et al.,"Comparison of Three User Interface Proposals," UNIX International, San Francisco, 1989.

Lautz, K.A., and W.I. Nowicki, "Structured Graphics for Distributed Systems", *ACM Transactions on Graphics* 3, no. 1, 1984, pp. 23-51.

Mace, T., "Unix International and User Interface Technology," keynote address at Xhibition89, Boston, June 1989.

Myers, B.A., "Window Interfaces: A Taxonomy of Window Manager User Interfaces," *IEEE Computer Graphics and Application* 8, no. 5, September 1988.

——"User Interface Toolkits: Present and Future," in Phillips, R.L., *SIGGRAPH '88 Panel Proceedings,* ACM, New York, 1989.

Open Software Foundation, *OSF/Motif Window Manager and OSF/Motif Toolkit Preliminary Functional Specification,* OSF, Cambridge, MA, 1990.

Pountain, D., "The X Window System," *Byte* 14, no. 1, January 1989, pp. 353-360.

Rao, R., and S. Wallace, "The X Toolkit: The Standard Toolkit for X Version 11," in *Proceedings of the Usenix Summer Conference,* Usenix, Berkeley, CA, 1987.

Rosenthal, D.S.H., "X Window System, Version 11
Inter-Client Communication Conventions Manual," in
Farrell, J., and D. A. LavaLee, "User Interfaces as
Window Systems: Architecture and Implementation,"
CHI '89 Tutorial Course Notes no. 25, ACM/SIGCHI,
ACM, New York, 1988, pp. 115-159.

Scheifler, R.W., and J. Gettys, J., "The X Window
System," *ACM Transactions on Graphics,* ACM,
New York, 1986.

Smith, D.C., et al., "Designing the Star User Interface,"
Byte 6, no. 4, April 1982, pp. 242-282.

Stern, H., "Comparison of Window Systems," *Byte* 12,
no. 11, November 1988, pp. 265-272.

Sun Microsystems, *OPEN LOOK Graphical User
Interface Functional Specification, Release 1.0*,
Mountain View, CA, 1989.

Swick, R.R., and M.S. Ackerman, "The X Toolkit:
More Bricks for Building User Interfaces or Widgets
for Hire," in *Proceedings of the Usenix Winter
Conference,* Usenix, Berkeley, CA, 1988, pp. 221-228.

Thompson, T., and N. Baran, "The NeXT Computer,"
Byte 13, no.11, November 1988, pp. 158-175.

Varhol, P.D., "OPEN LOOK," *MIPS* , July 1989,
pp. 40-44.

Index

A

Accent operating system *56*, 57
Adjacent hue *79*
Adobe 16
Aerial perspective 18
Aesthetic 19, 63
Alphanumerics 41
Ambient-light 87
American National Standards Institute (ANSI) 64
Angles 57
Animation 21, 60, 107, 129
Apollinaire 44
Appearance 118, 125
Apple 57, 195
Apple Lisa 52, 57
Apple Macintosh 13, 45, 52, 137, 139.
See also Macintosh
Application 150, 158
Application menu 199, 202
Application window 193, 200
Architectural design 6
Architecture 15, 19
Arithmetic 99
Arithmetic line charts 102
Ascender *32*, 35
AutoDesk 5
Axes 101

M

Author's Biography

Aaron Marcus

Aaron Marcus is an internationally recognized authority on graphic design for electronic publishing and user interfaces, especially chart, form, document, icon, color, and screen design. He has given tutorials on these subjects at annual conferences of the National Computer Graphics Association (NCGA), The Association for Computing Machinery's (ACM) Special Interest Group on Computer-Human Interaction (SIGCHI), and ACMs Special Interest Group on Graphics and Interaction (SIGGRAPH), in addition to tutorials at companies in the United States, Australia, Canada, Finland, Israel, Singapore, and Japan.

As founder and principal of Aaron Marcus and Associates, he has designed and critiqued computer graphics presentations, user interfaces, templates, and documentation for Apple, Ashton-Tate, Commodore-Amiga, Computervision, DEC, DuPont, Eastman Kodak, Equitable Life Insurance, General Motors, Hewlett-Packard, IBM, MCC, McDonnell-Douglas, Microsoft, Motorola, NCR, Pacific Bell, Reuters, Scitex, U.S. Department of Defense, U.S. Department of Energy, 3M, and many other organizations and institutions.

In addition to winning graphic design awards for excellence in visual communication over the past twenty years from organizations such as the Art Director's Club of New York, The Type Director's Club of New York, the Society of Publication Designers, and Industrial Design Magazine, Mr. Marcus has published more than fifty articles on graphic design for computer graphics in technical and professional journals. He authored the essay "Color: A Tool for Computer Graphics Communication" in the *The Computer Image* and co-authored *Human Factors and Typography for More Readable Programs,* both published by Addison-Wesley Publishing Co. Mr. Marcus received a B.A. in Physics from Princeton University (1965) and a B.F.A. and an M.F.A. in Graphic Design from Yale University Art School (1968). He has programmed and designed computer graphics since 1967 and has taught graphic design for computer graphics since 1970.